GERMAN-JEWISH POPULAR CULTURE BEFORE THE HOLOCAUST

David A. Brenner examines how Jews in Central Europe developed one of the first "ethnic" or "minority" cultures in modernity. Not exclusively "German" or "Jewish," the experiences of German-speaking Jewry in the decades prior to the Third Reich and the Holocaust were also negotiated in encounters with popular culture, particularly the novel, the drama and mass media.

Despite recent scholarship, the misconception persists that Jewish Germans were bent on assimilation. Although subject to compulsion, they did not become solely "German," much less "European." Yet their behavior and values were by no means exclusively "Jewish," as the Nazis or other antisemites would have it. Rather, the German Jews achieved a peculiar synthesis between 1890 and 1933, developing a culture that was not only "middle-class" but also "ethnic." In particular, they reinvented Judaic traditions by way of a hybridized culture.

Based on research in German, Israeli, and American archives, *German-Jewish Popular Culture before the Holocaust* addresses many of the genres in which a specifically German-Jewish identity was performed, from the Yiddish theater and Zionist humor all the way to sensationalist memoirs and Kafka's own kitsch. This middle-class ethnic identity encompassed and went beyond religious confession and identity politics. In focusing principally on German-Jewish popular culture, this groundbreaking book introduces the beginnings of "ethnicity" as we know it and live it today.

David A. Brenner is lecturer in Liberal Arts at the University of Houston.

ROUTLEDGE JEWISH STUDIES SERIES
Series Editor: Oliver Leaman
University of Kentucky

Studies which are interpreted to cover the disciplines of history, sociology, anthropology, culture, politics, philosophy, theology, and religion, as they relate to Jewish affairs. The remit includes texts that have as their primary focus issues, ideas, personalities, and events of relevance to Jews, Jewish life, and the concepts that have characterized Jewish culture both in the past and today. The series is interested in receiving appropriate scripts or proposals.

MEDIEVAL JEWISH PHILOSOPHY
An introduction
Dan Cohn-Sherbok

FACING THE OTHER
The ethics of Emmanuel Levinas
Edited by Seán Hand

MOSES MAIMONIDES
Oliver Leaman

A USER'S GUIDE TO FRANZ ROSENZWEIG'S STAR OF REDEMPTION
Norbert M. Samuelson

ON LIBERTY
Jewish philosophical perspectives
Edited by Daniel H. Frank

REFERRING TO GOD
Jewish and Christian philosophical and theological perspectives
Edited by Paul Helm

JUDAISM, PHILOSOPHY, CULTURE
Selected studies by E. I. J. Rosenthal
Erwin Rosenthal

PHILOSOPHY OF THE TALMUD
Hyam Maccoby

FROM SYNAGOGUE TO CHURCH
The traditional design: its beginning, its definition, its end
John Wilkinson

HIDDEN PHILOSOPHY OF HANNAH ARENDT
Margaret Betz Hull

DECONSTRUCTING THE BIBLE
Abraham ibn Ezra's introduction to the Torah
Irene Lancaster

IMAGE OF THE BLACK IN JEWISH CULTURE
A history of the other
Abraham Melamed

FROM FALASHAS TO ETHIOPIAN JEWS
Daniel Summerfield

PHILOSOPHY IN A TIME OF CRISIS
Don Isaac Abravanel: defender of the faith
Seymour Feldman

JEWS, MUSLIMS AND MASS MEDIA
Mediating the 'other'
Edited by Tudor Parfitt with Yulia Egorova

JEWS OF ETHIOPIA
The birth of an elite
Edited by Emanuela Trevisan Semi and Tudor Parfitt

ART IN ZION
The genesis of national art in Jewish Palestine
Dalia Manor

HEBREW LANGUAGE AND JEWISH THOUGHT
David Patterson

CONTEMPORARY JEWISH PHILOSOPHY
An introduction
Irene Kajon

ANTISEMITISM AND MODERNITY
Innovation and continuity
Hyam Maccoby

JEWS AND INDIA
History, image, perceptions
Yulia Egorova

JEWISH MYSTICISM AND MAGIC
An anthropological perspective
Maureen Bloom

MAIMONIDES' *GUIDE TO THE PERPLEXED*
Silence and salvation
Donald McCallum

MUSCULAR JUDAISM
The Jewish body and the politics of regeneration
Todd Samuel Presner

JEWISH CULTURAL NATIONALISM
David Aberbach

THE JEWISH–CHINESE NEXUS
A meeting of civilizations
Edited by M. Avrum Ehrlich

GERMAN-JEWISH POPULAR CULTURE
BEFORE THE HOLOCAUST
Kafka's kitsch
David Brenner

GERMAN-JEWISH POPULAR CULTURE BEFORE THE HOLOCAUST

Kafka's kitsch

David A. Brenner

Routledge
Taylor & Francis Group

LONDON AND NEW YORK

First published 2008
by Routledge
2 Park Square, Milton Park, Abingdon, Oxon OX14 4RN

Simultaneously published in the USA and Canada
by Routledge
270 Madison Avenue, New York, NY 10016

Routledge is an imprint of the Taylor & Francis Group, an informa business

© 2008 David A. Brenner

Typeset in Times New Roman by
Taylor & Francis Books
Printed and bound in Great Britain by
Biddles Ltd, King's Lynn, Norfolk

British Library Cataloguing in Publication Data
A catalogue record for this book is available from the British Library

Library of Congress Cataloging-in-Publication Data
Brenner, David A., 1964–
German-Jewish popular culture before the Holocaust: Kafka's kitsch /
David A. Brenner.
p. cm. – (Routledge Jewish studies series)
Includes bibliographical references and index.
1. Jews in popular culture – Germany – History – 20th century. 2.
Jews – Germany – Intellectual life – 20th century. 3. Popular culture –
Germany. I. Title.
DS134.255.B74 2008
305.892'404309041 – dc22
2008002616

ISBN 10: 0-415-46323-8 (hbk)
ISBN 10: 0-203-89403-0 (ebk)

ISBN 13: 978-0-415-46323-2 (hbk)
ISBN 13: 978-0-203-89403-3 (ebk)

CONTENTS

Acknowledgements viii

Introduction: Identifying (with) German-Jewish popular culture 1

1 Between high and low, laughter and tears: making Yiddish theater "respectable" in turn-of-the-century Jewish Berlin 12

2 "*Schlemiel*, Shlimazel": a proto-postcolonialist satire of "Jews," "Blacks," and "Germans" 29

3 A German-Jewish hermaphrodite: or what sexology contributed to B'nai B'rith 41

4 Franz's folk(lore): Kafka's Jewish father complex 50

5 Pogrom in – Berlin? Working through the Weimar Jewish experience in popular fiction 63

6 After the "Schoah": performing German-Jewish symbiosis today 78

Notes 88
Bibliography 105
Index 116

ACKNOWLEDGEMENTS

I am grateful for the assistance I received at the various stages of writing this book.

My interest in Jewish popular culture has roots in family history. My grandfather Leo, born near Czernowitz, settled eventually in Los Angeles (or was it Hollywood? ...), and my father Larry, born in Los Angeles (or was it Hollywood?...) taught me as much about theater, film and popular song as my professors. He may not realize it, but he is an entertainment historian and a discerning critic.

I am still fortunate to have completed doctoral work at the University of Texas. There I have mentors from whom I continue to benefit, including John Hoberman, Janet Swaffar, Kirsten Belgum, Katherine Arens, Itzik Gottesman, Peter Hess, and others. Colleagues from my year at Cornell are (more than theoretically) present in my work, ranging from Leslie Adelson, David Bathrick, and Peter Hohendahl to Sander Gilman and Dominick LaCapra. At Kent State, I was sustained – despite the chill and the shoveling – by Sharon and Robert Bell, Mark Bracher, Ken Calkins, Ron Corthell, Ken Cushner, Manuel Fontes, Stevan Hobfoll, John and Suzy Jameson, Sean Martin, Bill and Françoise Massardier-Kenney, Molly Merryman, David Odell-Scott, Victor Papacosma, Mark Weber, and others.

In my year as Fulbright Senior Scholar at the University of Konstanz (Germany), I was nurtured (intellectually and otherwise) by Aleida and Jan Assmann, Séamus McClelland, Albrecht Koschorke, Andreas Kraft, Nina Kück, Heiner Wehrli, and the incomparable Leippi clan.

For their assistance in reading and critiquing various drafts of this book over many years, I am particularly indebted to: Mark Anderson, Steve Aschheim, Lawrence Baron, Sharon Bell, Michael Berkowitz, Russell Berman, John Bormanis, Daniel Boyarin, Jonathan Boyarin, Mark Bracher, Michael Brenner, Iris Bruce, Judith Butler, Stanley Corngold, William Donahue, John Efron, Linda Feldman, Manuel Fontes, Mark Gelber, Sander Gilman, Itzik Gottesman, Jeffrey Grossman, Peter Haas, Geoffrey Hartman, Hilary Herzog, Todd Herzog, Susannah Heschel, John Hoberman, Hans-Otto Horch, Paula Hyman, Achim Jaeger, Anton Kaes, Sue Kassouf, Anthony Kauders, Hillel Kieval, Martin Jay, Peter Jelavich,

Robin Judd, Marion Kaplan, Alan Levenson, Glenn Levine, Dagmar Lorenz, Mike Luetzeler, Sean Martin, Françoise Massardier-Kenney, Paul Mendes-Flohr, Leslie Morris, George Mosse, Howard Needler, Diana Orendi, Jeff Peck, Derek Penslar, Keith Pickus, Paul Reitter, Karen Remmler, Ben Robinson, Eric Santner, Hinrich Seeba, Glenn Sharfman, Hermann Simon, Scott Spector, David Suchoff, Janet Swaffar, David Weinberg, Seth Wolitz, Jack Zipes, and Jeremy Zwelling. And in closing this long list: many others deserve special mention, perhaps even those who provided resistance by placing stumbling blocks in my path to completing this work. Needless to say, any errors which remain are my responsibility.

I have the pleasure now to thank those institutions which provided generous fellowships at crucial stages for the research on this project: the German Academic Exchange Service (DAAD), the Alexander von Humboldt Foundation, the Andrew W. Mellon Foundation, and the National Endowment for the Humanities.

I continue to esteem the extraordinary service of the librarians and archivists with whom I have worked. I received assistance and hospitality at the following archives: the Central Zionist Archives (Jerusalem), the Archives for History of the Jewish People (Jerusalem), the Leo Baeck Institute (New York), the Bundesarchiv (Berlin). Among the libraries I worked in are: the Jewish National and University Library in Jerusalem, the Bibliothek der jüdischen Gemeinde (Berlin), the library of the Jewish Theological Seminary (New York City) , Cornell University Libraries (Ithaca), and the Bibliothek der Universität Konstanz. At Kent State, thanks go out especially to Melissa Spohn, Mark Weber, and the outstanding circulation staff.

Portions of this book have been previously published in an earlier form. A portion of chapter 1 appeared as "Making Jargon Respectable: The Reception of Yiddish Theater in Pre-Hitler Germany" in the Yearbook of the Leo Baeck Institute 42 (1997): 51–66. Part of chapter 3 appeared as "Re (-)dressing the 'German-Jewish': A Jewish Hermaphrodite in Wilhelmine Germany," in Borders, Exiles, and Diasporas, Elazar Barkan and Marie-Denise Shelton, eds. (Stanford: Stanford University Press, 1998): 32–45. Portions of Chapter 4 appeared as "Uncovering the Father: Kafka, Judaism, and Homoeroticism" in Kafka, Zionism, and Beyond, Mark Gelber, ed. (Tübingen: Niemeyer, 2004): 207–218. And a large part of chapter 5 appeared as "Reconciliation Before Auschwitz: The Weimar Jewish Experience in Popular Fiction" in Evolving Jewish Identities in German Culture: Borders and Crossings, Linda Feldman and Diana Orendi, eds. (Westport, CT: Greenwood/Praeger, 2000): 45–61. I thank the respective editors and publishers for permission to revise and reprint my work.

Lastly, I am grateful to Oliver Leaman. To work under the guidance of such a serious editor and scholar has been my privilege. Special thanks are also due to the wonderful people at Routledge, in particular Joe Whiting and Paola Celli.

ACKNOWLEDGEMENTS

For support and the many phone calls, I am blessed with the friendship of Glenn and Ursula Levine, Achim Jaeger and Anne Cerbe, and Stan and Katie Kelfer Taylor. And without my family, this project would truly never have been completed, much less started. Words are not adequate in expressing my thanks to my sister Lynn, my brother-in-law Scott, my father Larry and my stepmother Gloria. The book is dedicated to my mother, Gladys, of blessed memory, and my daughter, Rafaela, of blessed presence.

INTRODUCTION
Identifying (with) German-Jewish popular culture

I

Even though Franz Kafka (1883–1924) is better known as a modernist writer of the highest caliber, he was also fond of popular culture, especially the cinema. While some artists and intellectuals seemed almost to fear the new medium, Kafka was virtually obsessed with it.[1] In time, going to the movies became *the* escapist activity for this notably ascetic writer. Film was able to tear him away from his desk, from the fever of literature, from writing as "a form of prayer." [2] Kafka even incorporated film images in his fiction. Preferring the cinema to the legitimate drama, Kafka moved from Prague to Berlin in the final years of his life, referring to the latter's "easy life, great opportunities [and] *pleasurable diversions.*"[3]

More typically, iconic German-Jewish writers such as Kafka are viewed through a post-Holocaust lens, lending them an aura of tragic nobility. Yet Kafka died in 1924, years before the Nazis came to power. Nor was he, as some still mistakenly presume, murdered in a concentration camp. On the basis of these and similar anachronisms, one expert on Kafka has recently called for a reassessment of German-Jewish studies, maintaining that an unreflective identification with Jewish victims by German intellectuals and Germanists "has consistently skewed their professional judgments about Jewish as well as German issues."[4]

"Backshadowing" is a term given to this form of hindsight.[5] Such hindsight, projected backwards onto history, tends to uncover teleology – where contingency is more the rule. If the Holocaust is likened to an earthquake, wrote Jean-François Lyotard, then it destroyed "not only the landscape but all the seismographs."[6] As a consequence, the tone of even scholarly discussion about German Jewry is rarely free of polemics. In the most infamous instance, Gershom Scholem diagnosed the "German-Jewish dialogue" as a one-way monologue spoken *by* Jews *at* non-Jews in Germany. Yet what even Zionist moderates such as Scholem portrayed as a nearly masochistic fantasy of "German-Jewish symbiosis" has also been characterized as the essential progressive project of modernity and/or a core paradigm of secularization in the West.

"We must understand the triumphs in order to understand the tragedy." That is the judgment of historian Fritz Stern on the extraordinary long-term success of the acculturated Jews of Germany.[7] As Amos Elon concludes in the most recent historical survey of Jewish Germans: "For long periods, they had cause to believe in their ultimate integration, as did most Jews elsewhere in Western Europe, in the United States, and even in czarist Russia. It was touch and go almost to the end."[8] If we in the post-Holocaust era can acknowledge that the devastation was unpredictably uncertain, the "assimilationist self-hatred" attributed to Jewish Germans can be revealed as a discourse and instrument of ideology – and not a self-delusion or political "bad faith."

Similarly, within "British" or "Birmingham School" cultural studies, resistance to acculturation was conceived not as triumphant or even as liberating, but simply a recognition that hegemony was rarely total. To Raymond Williams, the founder of this approach, there was always struggle and contestation even when the dominant culture was victorious. In contrast to the total dominion implicit in (overdetermined) ideological concepts of base and superstructure, Williams conceived of alternative and oppositional cultures as part of a hegemony that continually had to be reiterated to face new challenges. According to Stuart Hall, William's *de facto* successor, popular culture "is one of the sites where this struggle for and against a culture of the powerful is engaged: it is also the stake to be won or lost in the struggle...the arena of consent and resistance."[9] Then Hall added, in an *aperçu* rarely cited: "That is why 'popular culture' matters. Otherwise, to tell you the truth, I don't give a damn about it."[10]

II

Mass-mediated culture for German-Jewish audiences around 1900 was "middlebrow" culture, consisting of books, concerts, and theater as well as the emerging media of film, the phonograph, and the magazine. As for other Westerners, a middle-class popular culture provided the material out of which German-Jewish identities were forged, identities articulated not only in terms of ethnicity but also class, gender, and nationality. The images and stories most often cited or "performed" by Jewish Germans shaped their view of the world and their deepest values, what they considered "good" or "bad," "familiar" and "foreign." These media – themselves mediated through language and other signifying practices – supplied Jewish Germans with the symbols, myths, and resources through which their identities were formed. By instructing them in how to conform to dominant systems of norms, values, and institutions, the middle-class media were constitutive and unavoidable for German-Jewish culture-makers.

Living an identity that was hyphenated or hybridized (before those terms became popular), Jews in the German cultural sphere both created and consumed a popular culture. Kafka, in particular, was engaged in a sub-culture that differed from the German-Jewish mainstream, one that enabled resistive identities defining themselves against standard models. For all his emulation of Goethe, Kleist, and other canonical writers, Kafka continued to read devotedly the little Prague Jewish cultural weekly *Selbstwehr*, even while traveling.[11] At the same time, Jews in history have typically defined themselves as a people or religious group with an identity essentially different from other peoples or religious groups. Yet Jewish identity, as it has been practiced and performed, has been more fluid than fixed, more heterogeneous than homo-geneous. In the last decades, many theorists have challenged all "essentializ-ing" criteria, arguing that identities are not functions of nature but cultural constructs. For others, identity has become a differentiated process of multi-ple identification, subject to regular confirmation and occasional revision.

Neither exclusively ethnic nor religious, Jewish identity may seem to differ little from other "identities," if "identity" is conceived as a shifting combi-nation of identifications variously enacted. Yet Jewish identity has almost always been a minority affair, evolving according to the complex power relations between Jews and the majority cultures where they found them-selves. Similarly, the focus of theoretical discussions of Jewish identity has often depended upon the audience being addressed, whether it be major-itarian or minoritarian, popular or academic, and so on. For audiences may vary according to factors of ethnicity, class, gender, and nationality (at least).

As a Jew, an educator, a man, and an American (at least), I wish with this book to address an audience interested in interdisciplinary approaches to the study of society and culture. In the process, I will also utilize categories of literary and cultural theory to the degree which that theory bears upon the performance of identities. This I believe is necessary in order to tease out the complexities of Jewish identities in modern Germany – the focus of this book – and, by extension, to almost anywhere Jews have lived. Since the onset of emancipation and Enlightenment, Jewish identity has become truly multiple: to be a Jew in the modern West means to be at once a Jew and also something else. Jewish identity is in this sense emblematic of modern identity, and vice versa.

It is a major contention of this book that such matters have not been addressed in their complexity.[12] In fact, one could identify its project as placing the *differences* among Jews at the center of debate, especially where those differences – as in studies of German Jewry – have gone unpursued. This I find is best accomplished through a case study approach. Attempts to problematize identity, after all, involve different contexts. They also inevi-tably involve the respective interpreter's positionality. For our judgments of writers, texts, and contexts – and what constitute them – are themselves formed by contingencies in our lives and times.

So greater reflection can do little harm. The analytical categories that have preoccupied history and theory in the last thirty years ought to be applied in our encounters with German-Jewish narratives today. There is already a growing interest in German Judaica, much of it generated in the fields of North American German Studies and Jewish Studies. Yet, while this interest is for the most part felicitous, some scholars and writers still fail to make explicit where they stand methodologically. In their criteria for what constitutes identity, many in Jewish Studies and/or German Studies have not engaged in recognizable conversations taking place throughout the Anglo-American academy. In fact, the tangled relationship of identity and the subject is itself informed by an expanding literature.[13] This important (if jargon-ridden) body of work aims to disrupt received dichotomies of essence versus accident, agency versus structure, and universalism versus particularism. Although one does not need to cite specific writings of Michel Foucault, Judith Butler, or Stuart Hall, theoretical debates – some more, some less intense – surrounding feminism, Marxism, psychoanalysis, gender studies, cultural theory, and postcolonial studies have much to add to the study of Jewish (and German) identity formation.[14]

In this book, I want to begin to address Jews and their self-representations in the German cultural sphere and elsewhere by juxtaposing the political demands for identity (of an individual or a group) with critiques of essentialist conceptions of identity.[15] How have the urgencies of emancipatory politics conflicted with or engaged psychoanalytic and poststructuralist critiques of the subject's identity? And in what terms should critics and theorists approach Jewish-German culture in light of "the oppressive as well as energizing effects of essentializing tropes of identity"?[16]

To synthesize these at times conflicting moments of discourse is a task perhaps suited for philosophers. The considerations that follow agree with the Foucauldian insight that "all identities operate through exclusion, through the discursive reconstruction of a constitutive outside and the production of abjected and marginalized subjects."[17] For, if we reconceive identity as an *effect*, that is as produced or generated, it "opens up possibilities of 'agency' that are insidiously foreclosed by positions that take identity categories as foundation and fixed."[18]

It is necessary, then, to be circumspect. We should employ the same criteria in identity theory that we use when analyzing anything else. This means in particular avoiding the impulse to simplify where the complexity of the matter is evident. To be sure, most people are not eager to hear about the nuanced distinctions that academics are accustomed to making. But in matters as dense and complex as identity – collective as well as individual – humility is of the essence. And one does not necessarily need theory to grasp how unachievable certainty can be.

III

In the following considerations on German-Jewish identities, it is compelling to cite Judith Butler, if only because her work on subject formation regularly problematizes our understanding of identity, agency, and history. It may be no accident that her theories about how gender is performed have influenced artists, filmmakers, and political activists as well as philosophers and other academics. In the final chapter of this book, I address the applicability of Butler's theories, in all their contradictions, to German-Jewish writing. For the most part, however, I will adhere to a more colloquial usage of "performance," one that intersects with important work being done in the less philosophical realm of (British) cultural studies.

Specifically, I am arguing that Jews in Germany had at their disposal a corpus of texts and discourses that informed, indeed *per*formed, their Jewish identities. No longer availing themselves chiefly of Talmud, Midrash, and related genres, they began in the nineteenth century to mediate their identities by way of novels, histories, cinema, theater, and jokes – in short, by way of *popular culture*. This culture became the highly complex site of their identity formation, as it had become for other Central and Western Europeans of the epoch. For the late nineteenth century was a turning point in the history of how culture was produced, consumed, and otherwise disseminated. At the same time, it preceded the "homogenization" of audiences allegedly perpetrated by "mass culture."

In the twentieth century, the Anglo-American concepts of "popular culture" and "mass culture" – although not as pejorative as the German term *Kitsch* (or the Yiddish *shund*) – suggest a negative judgment about a work's artistic merit and its audience. Within the fields of German and Jewish cultural studies, lowbrow culture is often still interpreted in the shadow of Theodor W. Adorno and Max Horkheimer. Their *Dialectic of Enlightenment* (completed in 1944, published in 1947) linked all forms of popular culture, from jazz and movies to detective fiction, to a near-monolithic "culture industry."[19] In the conclusion to their famous essay, one reads that "[t]he triumph of advertising in the culture industry is that consumers feel compelled to buy and use its products even though they see through them."[20] What is troped here as paradoxical emerged from two thinkers of German-Jewish background who rendered the dominant genres of popular entertainment part of a sinister yet (oddly) transparent campaign of diversion, manipulation, and "reification."[21]

To postwar American Germanists, many of them newly exiled Jewish Germans, this ideology of mass culture had a distinct appeal in the immediate aftermath of horrors committed in the name of Germany.[22] Some of them, not unlike Adorno and Horkheimer, seemed nostalgic after Auschwitz for an ideology of *Bildung* ("formation" or "cultivation"). Yet a new generation of historians, including Anson Rabinbach and Steven

Aschheim, has since revised the notion that *Bildung* was some sort of time-less transcendent, particularly for German Jews.[23] Nor were the disasters of National Socialism and the Holocaust inevitable, even if at times the nine-teenth-century invention of a distinctively national German culture seemed to hint at its twentieth-century excesses.[24]

While Adorno and Horkheimer's chapter on "The Culture Industry" ostensibly ended without hope of liberation from "mass deception," its unpublished conclusion remained faithful to the possibilities of the Enlightenment for autonomous subjectivity: "It depends on human beings themselves whether they will...awaken from a nightmare that only threatens to become actual as long as they believe in it."[25] To be sure, these two phi-losophers were so highly "assimilated" that their identities were scarcely informed by what I refer to as German-Jewish popular culture.[26] But theirs was a kind of secondary reaction formation, a possible response (among many) to perceived deficits in nineteenth-century German and German-Jewish culture. Indeed, analyzed more closely, popular culture may always have been the necessary basis for what is termed "high culture." As sug-gested above, many intellectuals in the modernist movement displayed a supercilious, alarmist view of mass democracy, perceiving culture and art to be constantly endangered by the "lowbrow."[27]

In a contrary tendency, Raymond Williams and other practitioners of British (or Birmingham School) cultural studies have at times tended to *overlook* popular culture's "dark side," just as the remaining disciples of Adorno and Horkheimer omit its heritage of dissent. But one need not make an absolute choice between ideology critique, on the one hand, and Williams, on the other.[28] The industrialization of culture and communica-tion, highly advanced though it most assuredly is, has itself not been fully realized as prophesied by Adorno and Horkheimer. This is not only valid for present-day America or Germany but was also true in the nascent days of the German-Jewish "culture industry" in the late nineteenth century. In ways not foreseen by the early "Frankfurt School," the expansion and diversifi-cation of the culture industry has opened up spaces in the public sphere where a non-manipulative, even critical, employment of the means of cul-tural communication has become possible. Culture, in short, has become the site of critical resistance (or "negativity," to use Adorno's term) as well as ideological manipulation, both in Germany and in German Studies.[29]

The same holds for *ethnic* culture as a site of potential resistance or autonomous performance – a major contention of this book. Miriam Hansen argues, in a perceptive essay on the public sphere and the necessity of counterpublics, that

> [c]ommunity and counterpublic are "authentic" only when they know themselves as rhetoric, as tropes of impossible authenticity that reinvent the so-called promise of community through synthetic

images…and the extent to which they admit difference and differentiation within their own borders…[and] are capable of accepting multiply-determined identities and identifications.[30]

Hansen thus reveals how a middle-class counterpublic, one with some degree of self-awareness, is a distinct possibility. For the moment when a spectator moves from being "the hypothetical point of address" to being a member of "a plural, social audience" can produce surprises.[31] Jacqueline Bobo's analysis of black women viewers of *The Color Purple* (dir. Steven Spielberg, 1985) is a case in point. The ways in which these spectators identified with elements of the film invoked their experience as a historical minority in "ways quite unparalleled in dominant culture – a far cry from the dismissal of the film by critics."[32]

Until recently, German Jewry was known less for its ethnic experiences and more for its valuable "contributions" to modern German *and* modern Judaic cultures. Nonetheless, it also participated in the invention of one of the first middle-class and minority cultures in the modern West. Yet, taking a cursory glance at the last fifty years of scholarship, one might conclude that most German-speaking Jews in pre-Holocaust Europe preferred philosophy to popular culture, lyric poetry to ladies' journals, the Jewish youth movement to joke-books, and Schnitzler and Mahler to comic theater and cabaret. Long after becoming a Zionist and the pre-eminent scholar of Jewish mysticism, Gershom (born Gerhard) Scholem was still embarrassed that his parents owned "Jewish joke-books."[33] Other evidence, however, suggests that Scholem's coreligionists in Germany and Austria did not universally eschew popular Jewish culture. The idea that German Jews were lacking in humor and averse to pleasure still abides in the stereotype of the *yekke* (written *Jecke* in German). And, according to pundits, a Jew in Germany must have been bent on assimilation – or worse, apostasy.

German Jews, even the non-observant and non-Zionist, were familiar with and interested in things Jewish. One goal of studying how Jewish Germans created and consumed German-Jewish popular culture is to learn how this culture *constituted* their sentiments and values. The present book poses the question of how subjects accept or resist the hegemony of majority cultures. To what degree did German-Jewish popular culture reveal the crucial ambivalence of modernity, not only in its potential to be adopted and co-opted, but also in its capacity for resistance or counterhegemony?

In practicing this type of cultural studies, *German-Jewish Popular Culture before the Holocaust* also echoes those voices seeking "to make the critique of canon formation an integral part of interpretive and evaluative investigation."[34] A key goal of studying how Jews consumed German-Jewish – and German – culture is to learn how their "Jewishness" affected their beliefs, perceptions, values, and interpretations, as these were experienced in the contexts of family and work, in the private and public spheres. There

were clearly moments of resistance to the imposition of cultural homo-
geneity as well as the hegemony of the majority culture. Thus, to what
extent did German Jews identify with Jewish concerns – and what were
those Jewish concerns? What were the factors and processes involved in
this identification? And: to what extent were high-, low-, and middlebrow
culture capable of providing German Jews with an "ethnic identity" or
"imagined community"?

IV

In the first chapter, "Between high and low, laughter and tears," I examine
the reception of East European Jewish culture by Kafka's German-Jewish
contemporaries. In particular, the chapter considers Yiddish theater as performed in Germany around 1900. When Kafka proposed to his (then)
fiancée that she catch a performance of his friend Jitzchak Löwy's Yiddish
dramatic troupe in the Jewish ghetto of Berlin (the *Scheunenviertel*), he again
proved himself less of a snob than we might expect. His warning to Felice
Bauer that the theater in question might be "shabby" could easily have been
misunderstood. But Kafka was by that point of his life a fan of Yiddish
theater – and rarely attended "legitimate theater" thereafter. Prior to the
"Jewish renaissance" of the 1920s, Kafka was veritably obsessed with
Eastern Jewish culture. In contrast to the mainstream German drama and its
depiction of Jews, Yiddish theater for "Yekkes" (i.e., *German* Jews) was
ironic and bittersweet, a merging of high and low culture, laughter with
tears.

In the following chapter, I examine the role of Jewish self-parody in Jewish
nationalist circles. Prior to World War I and Kafka's haunting *In the Penal
Colony*, German-speaking Jews were using irony to address European
"colonialism" in Palestine and elsewhere. In the first issue (1903) of the
Zionist-sponsored *Der Schlemiel: Ein illustriertes jüdisches Witzblatt* (The
Schlemiel: An Illustrated Jewish Humor Magazine), a satirical column was
introduced as a way of commenting on new controversies such as Ahad
Ha'am's "cultural Zionist" challenge to the politically oriented Zionist
organization. Titled "Briefe aus Neu-Neuland" (Letters from New-
Newland) – a pun on Theodor Herzl's controversial utopian work
Altneuland (Old-New Land) – this series of parodies featured a Ugandan
chieftain who converts to Orthodox Judaism and Religious Zionism. The
objective of the Western-born but Eastern-oriented Jews behind these letters
was to draw analogies between (European) "Jews" and (African) "Blacks."
In doing so, they wished to attract a Westernized, acculturated Jewish audience to an agenda of public, "open" Jewishness. Western Jews were in effect
asked to become "too Jewish" and, in the process of legitimizing the culture
and humor traditions of East European Jewry, *Schlemiel* became respectable
and rather well-known. While recent postcolonial criticism has been marked

by a comic restraint verging on reverence, none other than Homi Bhabha has specifically recognized *Jewish* self-irony as a (self-preserving) form of ethnic identification.

Chapter Three, "A German-Jewish hermaphrodite: or what sexology contributed to B'nai B'rith," examines gender and sexuality as "entertainment" in a bestselling memoir of 1907, which also served as the basis for films made in 1912 and 1919. *From a Man's Girl Years* is the autobiography of Karl Baer (pseudonym "N. O. Body") who, after his 1907 transgendering procedure (one of the first such operations ever), went on to serve as the director of the B'nai B'rith Lodges of Berlin. By all accounts a gifted and model Jewish functionary, he immigrated to Palestine in September 1938. Despite his importance in German-Jewish cultural life, Karl Baer had once been the same legal person, i.e., occupying the same body, as Martha Baer, a highly accomplished journalist, feminist, and Zionist. Baer's memoir uncovers how the concept of "self-hatred" a century ago was already a rhetorical phenomenon, a trope to appeal to (Jewish) middle-class readers. *From a Man's Girl Years* is thus the product of a complicated dialectic between intertextual and social factors.

A similar differentiated approach to ethnic, gender, and sexual boundaries is deployed in the following chapter on Kafka's own writings and multiple border crossings. There, I explore directly Kafka's own *kitsch*, his adaptations of popular (especially Eastern) Jewish culture. These included reworkings of popularized Kabbalah, especially early Hasidism, as mediated to Kafka by friends (Jiří Langer, Yitzchak Löwy) and through reading and other personal encounters (e.g., with Martin Buber, *the* middlebrow mediator of Hasidic tales). It was this hybrid Jewish mysticism – Kabbalah itself already marked as heretical and counterhegemonic – which rendered it possible for Kafka to reconfigure his own private Judaism and (even less well-known) gender ambivalence in works ranging from "The Judgment" (1912) all the way to *The Castle* (composed in the early 1920s).

Chapter Five, "Pogrom in – *Berlin*? Working through the Weimar Jewish experience in popular fiction," analyzes German-Jewish popular culture in the installment (or serial) novels published between 1922 and 1923 in the most widely circulated Jewish newspaper of Weimar Germany, the *Israelitisches Familienblatt* (*Israelite Family Journal*). Like other mass media, this "family journal" (published weekly in Hamburg, Frankfurt, and Berlin between 1898 and 1938) has rarely been analyzed by historians of German-speaking Jewry. This neglect is conspicuous, for the *Israelitisches Familienblatt* was *the* best-selling Jewish periodical in early twentieth-century Germany, reaching at least 15 percent of the potential Jewish market in the country – a high figure for any mass publication. Yet while purporting to understand German-Jewish lives and mentalities between 1918 and 1933, historians have omitted not only those media most popular with Weimar Jewry, but also the fictions that appeared between their pages. Representative

9

serial novels provide special insight into the self-understanding of Jews in Germany. And, by providing their targeted constituencies with the illusion of "community," a rhetorically constructed "ethnic" Jewish identity, these fictions made possible consensus amidst crisis for Jews in the early Weimar Republic.

As suggested throughout the book, theories of performativity should be added to the exploration for alternatives to standard accounts of a German-Jewish "symbiosis." In a concluding chapter on German-Jewish writing after Auschwitz, I examine a set of representations from recent fictions by writer Maxim Biller. One of the best-known contemporary writers in Germany, Biller was born in 1960 in Prague and has resided since 1970 in the Federal Republic. In particular, I juxtapose Judith Butler's theories with Biller's self-reflective stories, demonstrating how the latter draw attention to the constructedness of the post-Shoah negative symbiosis.

V

The theorist Jonathan Elmer, in a book on affect in modern mass culture, has argued that

> once popular culture is seen as a process of mediation rather than essentially an object, once it is seen as the very ground of cultural logic rather than a single, if inchoate element of the social horizon, then these dynamics of figurations and representation require a more supple approach to literary and cultural form.[35]

The representations and reflections that follow on German-Jewish popular culture as the field of play for consent and resistance move in the modest direction of providing just such a "more supple approach." To be sure, the notion of identity as both pleasurable and ideological provides a starting point for understanding German-Jewish subject formation. At the same time, modern cultural judgments are dominated by three basic approaches: (1) an "*art* discourse" in which the "ideal of cultural experience is *transcendence*"; (2) a "*folk* discourse" in which the "ideal of cultural experience is *integration*"; and (3) a "*pop* discourse" that provides "routinized pleasures... a play of desire and discipline."[36]

This final discourse, I contend, was already at work among turn-of-the-century German Jewry. While seldom strongly oppositional or resistant, this mediation process (or "cultural logic") is precisely what is meant in this book by *German-Jewish popular culture*. For German-speaking Jews, nearly a century ago, generated new combinations of aesthetic judgment and style while at the same time revising their ethnic, class, and gender affiliations. These were in turn reinscribed and reconfigured in new and different ways.

10

The participation of German Jews in such developments is thus another reminder of how far – and how far *back* – cultural theory must go to catch up with the culture-makers it studies. In closing, a *caveat* about cultural studies, which of late has become "shorthand for all political approaches to the study of literature, including various attempts of the past 30 years to bring issues of gender, race, class, and sexuality into the literary canon."[37] When used by hostile critics, cultural studies means reading literature solely in terms of its political context. One of my graduate school professors decried such work as "crude literary sociology." In the rhetoric of these detractors, aesthetics and cultural studies are reduced to a simplistic Manicheanism. Relying on an anthropological idea of culture, cultural studies seeks to make sense of the entire range of symbolic practices, texts, and belief systems in society. In concrete practice, cultural studies "involves a delicate balancing act between the macro and the micro and between the competing claims of textual and social analyses."[38] The following studies of German-Jewish popular culture seek to assist critics and historians in effectively balancing those claims.

1

BETWEEN HIGH AND LOW, LAUGHTER AND TEARS

Making Yiddish theater "respectable" in turn-of-the-century Jewish Berlin

Yet if you consider that laughter, laughing oneself to tears for sublime reasons, is the best thing we have [...], then you will be inclined as I am to count Kafka's loving fixations among the most readable things that world literature has ever generated.

Thomas Mann[1]

I

Observers of German Jewry have long used metaphors such as "symbiosis" to diagnose the status of modern Jewish identity in the German cultural sphere. Particularly since the Third Reich and the Holocaust, they have tended to be critical of the idea of "symbiosis." The notion that an individual could be, at one and the same time, "German" and "Jewish" was anathema in the wake of Nazi Germany. A good deal of post-1945 historiography laments those Jews living in Germany before World War II as "assimilationist," "self-hating," or just plain delusional.[2]

In particular, some historians censure German-Jewish attitudes and behavior toward other Jews, especially those from Eastern Europe (referred to as "Eastern Jews" or *Ostjuden* in this work).[3] Steven Aschheim's *Brothers and Strangers* (1982) represents one in a chorus of voices seeking to rescue the *Ostjude* from supposed German-Jewish domination. Aschheim demonstrates that German Jews, like their non-Jewish compatriots, adopted negative attitudes toward East European Jewry. He documents wide-scale production of negative stereotypes of *Ostjuden* by Jews and non-Jews. Yet, while duly noting that the idealization of *Ostjuden* took on cultic proportions after Martin Buber's earliest rehabilitations of the Hasidic tale, Aschheim's narrative and that of more strident critics of Western Jewry seemed to suggest that all attempts to reconcile Eastern and Western Jewish cultures were doomed from the start.[4]

While acknowledging that German Jews thought and behaved negatively toward their fellow Jews, the present chapter on the reception of Yiddish theater in pre-1933 Germany does not favor East European Jewry. Instead, it reveals how *both* Jewish groups – Eastern and Western – employed tried-and-true rhetorical tropes. Such a critical-cognitive approach complements approaches that conceive of Jewish identity before the Holocaust as pre-ordained by antisemitism.[5]

Now it is legitimate to ask whether the contempt of Western Jews for Eastern Jews might be categorized as "Jewish antisemitism." And certainly antisemitic attacks on Eastern Jews made German Jews look and feel under attack. According to the thesis of Jewish self-hatred, Western Jews hated not only their Eastern brethren but also, as a result of psychological projection, the Eastern Jew within *themselves*.[6] This assumption is that German Jews felt threatened by the prospect of "hordes" of Jewish aliens pouring across the eastern border. Even though Jewish migration to Germany never exceeded a few hundred per year until 1918 and even though the new Jewish immigrants were statistically insignificant in comparison to the host populations – the total number of *Ostjuden* who settled in Germany never exceeded 100,000 – their presence was immediately noticed by some government officials and most political opportunists. On this basis, Aschheim and others have argued that worried Jewish communities feared an antisemitic backlash and tried to keep the numbers of immigrants down or less visible.

Other historians, in the meantime, have presented evidence that the Jews in Germany responded proactively to the challenge posed by antisemitic attacks on Jews from the East. To be sure, some German Jews blamed Eastern Jews for antisemitism, pinpointing them as a source of shame or embarrassment. And the established Jews of the West may well have avoided contact with immigrant "Russians" and "Galicians," even treating them with condescension. But, writes one historian, the Jewish middle classes in Germany "also displayed compassion for the suffering of their coreligionists. ...[T]hey provided various types of support – legal aid, political support, and care for the needy....[F]rom the evidence at our disposal, it appears that their actions on behalf of the immigrants were incompatible with hatred."[7]

The point is not that Jews were incapable of mutual animosity. Centuries of "divide and conquer" practiced upon Jews, in the East and the West, had certainly left their mark. Nonetheless, the extent of their interactions and their cultural similarities suggest that a relationship existed – if not always a symbiotic one.

II

The present chapter looks at one such East–West Jewish encounter in early twentieth-century Berlin, viewed through the lens of one of the leading institutions that sought to build upon this relationship: the Berlin-based magazine *Ost und West*. As studies of popular Berlin theater, including Yiddish-language theater, are few and far between, scholars must rely on evidence of reception such as found in the Jewish and non-Jewish press.[8] *Ost und West* is an ideal source for evaluating this reception when considered not only as a textual apparatus extending over twenty years but also as a public relations enterprise promoting specific images of Jewishness to specific Jewish audiences.

For, despite the large body of research on stereotyping (largely social scientific) and on identity (largely poststructuralist), the *promotion* of positive and negative images has received less attention. Instead of employing value-laden categories such as "pathological" and "healthy," this chapter pursues how well or poorly stereotypes were marketed to specific social and cultural groups. Such an analysis implicitly acknowledges that stereotypes are protean, and this inherent instability of stereotypes enabled the image-makers behind *Ost und West* to appeal to different markets. The present study of Yiddish performance likewise affirms that stereotypes of the Jew differ from culture to culture, from era to era, and from institution to institution. The manipulation of historically specific stereotypes was the successful strategy behind *Ost und West*'s promotion of "ethnic" or "cultural" Jewishness to its German-speaking Jewish audiences.[9]

Through positive stereotyping of *Ostjuden* and negative stereotyping of *Westjuden*, *Ost und West* also provides valuable insight into what was regarded as "too Jewish" in this time and place, in particular suggesting how openly Jewish German Jewry was willing to be. For Yiddish theater in Germany was a challenge to those Jews who wished to remain "in the closet." In addition, Jewish popular culture such as cabaret or varieté did not first appear in Weimar-era Germany, in some re-fantasized "roaring 20s." Since 1901, *Ost und West* had already been hard at work promoting European Jewish culture to Jews in Germany and elsewhere. The magazine's program was to reverse Jewish "assimilation" in Western and Central Europe by constructing a "pro-ethnic" identity including East European forms of Jewishness. By focusing specifically on the reception of Yiddish theater in such a widespread publication, we can attempt to measure the extent to which Western Jews were truly interested in adopting elements of Eastern Jewishness at this time.

Even though *Ost und West* succeeded in creating a public sphere for "pan-Jewry" (*Gesamtjudentum*), it was confronted with challenges. East European Jews had been perceived negatively by many Western Jews and non-Jews since the Enlightenment. Since the late eighteenth century, an elite of intellectuals and policy-makers had called upon *Ostjuden* to become less Jewish. It was hoped instead that they would "regenerate" themselves into a group more like "the Germans," "the French," and so on. The *Ostjuden* were increasingly caricatured in a number of media and genres, from literature and the arts to the sciences. This trend was more widespread than ever when *Ost und West* began publication in 1901.

14

As a way to correct these negative images of East European Jews, *Ost und West* attempted to legitimize public expressions of Jewishness in the West. In this sense, the journal sought to "re-educate" Jews in Western Europe who knew little about Eastern Jewry. Despite its emphasis on re-education, however, *Ost und West* did not simply advance the interests of a Jewish nationalist avant-garde. Its founders knew that they would have to reflect the presuppositions of the broader Jewish audience if they were to attract more readers.

This task was well suited for Leo Winz (1876?–1952), the transplanted Ukrainian Jew and public relations man responsible for the magazine.[10] Winz was a veteran "image-maker" who had served between 1906 and 1908 as the head of public relations for the oldest major German advertising firm, Haasenstein & Vogler. To date, there is no biography of Winz or of his main associates at *Ost und West*.[11] Besides owning and investing in a range of businesses, Winz was also, between 1927 and 1934, the publisher of the largest Jewish newspaper in Germany, the *Gemeindeblatt der jüdischen Gemeinde zu Berlin* (The Communal News of the Jewish Federation of Berlin).

Judging by its wide circulation, *Ost und West* was a success. According to Winz's and independent estimates, the magazine had anywhere from 16,000 to 23,000 subscribers in the period between 1906 and 1914. These figures in turn can be multiplied by a factor of three (or more) to allow for circulation within cafés, reading rooms, and libraries. Hence, *Ost und West* reached at least 10 percent of the 625,000 Jews in Germany at its height. After the *Israelitisches Familienblatt* (*Israelite Family Journal*), published in Hamburg between 1898 and 1938, it was the best-selling German-Jewish publication of the epoch, proving there was a potential market in Germany for the magazine and its version of East European Jewish culture.[12]

To promote an *ethnic* Jewish identity, Winz published a rich variety of materials. In its first three years, *Ost und West* was best known for images that glorified Eastern Jewry. The journal thus differed visibly from competing German-Jewish publications in boldly asserting its Jewishness. As soon as the reader picked up an issue, he or she knew that the stories, essays, artwork, and photographs were provided by Jews, about Jews, and for Jews.[13] The very first issue (January 1901) featured an essay entitled "Jüdische Renaissance" by Martin Buber, a review of Robert Jaffé's *Ahasver* (1900) by Samuel Lublinski, a story by Isaac Leib Peretz in German translation, drawings by Ephraim Moses Lilien, and an article on the Hebrew language by Simon Bernfeld. In this and later issues, European Jewry was presented as having a proud ethnic heritage and diverse cultural traditions. Yet it was not enough to "repackage" the Eastern Jew, who remained dirty, poor, and superstitious in the minds of some Westerners. Rather, *Ostjuden* were to be subtly rehabilitated using the criteria of Western scholarship and aesthetics.

Such tensions are central in *Ost und West*'s first article glorifying the Yiddish language in March 1901. Here Fabius Schach, a close associate of Winz, shows a willingness to re-evaluate the term "Yiddish." While parodying the Western Yiddish dialect (or "Judeo-German") of Jewish horse and cattle dealers in Bavaria and Württemberg, Schach contends that the standard (Eastern) Yiddish language is more than a pidgin or creole.[14] Significantly, it meets the criteria of established (i.e., *Western*) languages and literatures: it is "organized," "grammatical," with a "strong periodical culture" and a literary output "more Realist than Romantic" in its style.[15]

Two months later, Schach again employs positive stereotyping to address the nature and history of the Yiddish theater: "The Jew has a fighting nature: he speaks and thinks dramatically....No people can speak so characteristically with eyes and fingers."[16] Yet Schach then labels Abraham Goldfaden (1840–1908) and the earliest Yiddish dramatists as purveyors of "low" culture. As if aware that he may be going too far in the opposite direction, he quickly issues an apologia:

> You cannot judge a people which is belated in its aesthetic education by the standards of [Gotthold Ephraim] Lessing's *Hamburg Dramaturgy*....We need theater for Russian Jews so that they may become culturally and aesthetically healthy....What is simple, beautiful and natural has not been understood by the Russian Jew. He has been raised for generations on *pilpul*, and he has been entertained by the "sport" of Talmud in lieu of flowers and sunlight. The soul of the Russian Jew is sick, perhaps even more sick than his body.[17]

This Zionist approach to Eastern Jewish culture, ultimately derived from Max Nordau's *Degeneration* (1892), was by no means grounded in Ashkenazic folk tradition. In line with the presuppositions of modern Western scholarship being produced by Jews and non-Jews, certain cultural forms and genres were to be accorded more respect. Language and legend, first valorized by Johann Gottfried von Herder (1744–1803), ranked highest, followed by poetry, sculpture, and painting. The essay rounded out this hierarchy of forms. Close to the bottom, in contrast, was non-classical drama, including the popular theatrical entertainments of East European Jews.

In line with its target audience, the typical ordering of genres in a given issue of *Ost und West* favored Western rather than Eastern Jewish readers. Even if many of the artists featured in the journal hailed from the East, they were repackaged for the Western Jewish reader. The only truly Eastern Jewish products in *Ost und West* were fiction, folklore, and the press summary, all of which appeared in German translation. The writers published most regularly – Peretz, Sholem Asch (1880–1957), Sholem Aleichem (1859–1916), and David Pinski (1872–1959) – were well known for their sensitivity to West European trends. In fact, most of the Eastern Jewish *belles-lettres* that appeared in *Ost und West* were decidedly humoristic and posed little or no obstacle to being understood by German-Jewish audiences.

The humoristic similarly dominated ethnic Jewish entertainment in *fin-de-siècle* Berlin. The following characterization of Yiddish theater, penned by the British-based, Rumanian-born, Jewish scholar Moses Gaster, was typical for the era: "It shows us our defects, which we have like all men, but not with a tendency to strike at our own immorality with...ill will, but only with an *ironic* spirit that does not wound us as we are wounded by representations on other stages where the Jew plays a degrading role."[18] For Gaster and other Jewish commentators, *irony* was the essential factor in nineteenth-century Eastern Jewish drama. In contrast to the mainstream German drama and its depiction of Jews, Yiddish theater for "Yekkes" (i.e., German Jews) was, as we shall see, a not-so-distant cousin of the Yiddish theater on the Second Avenue in New York City. Nor was it unrelated to the American but Yiddish-inflected performance culture of Eddie Cantor (in the 1930s), Mickey Katz (in the 1950s), and Lenny Bruce and the new wave of stand-up comics in the 1960s.[19]

This trajectory also corresponded to developments in nineteenth-century Yiddish fiction, specifically a movement from the *satire* of Mendele Moykher-Sforim (and other *maskilim*) to the post-pogrom *irony* of Sholem Aleichem. Yiddish theater in *fin-de-siècle* Germany was similarly ironic. Jewish comedy, in particular, was capable of a good measure of self-irony, to a "laughing *with* but not *at*." Early vaudeville in the United States also "poked fun at ethnic stereotypes – usually (but not always) their own."[20] This was a trend that was also taken up by the American Yiddish theater.

Interwoven with affection *vis-à-vis* the *shtetl*, though, Yiddish performance could call up previously repressed "strong emotions."[21] Kafka analyzed this concern in his "Speech on the Yiddish Language," a diagnosis which gets repeated in the history of Jewish encounters with reinvented traditions.[22] German-based Yiddish performances at times evinced reactions of shame, rendering them a "nostalgic domain reserved for our collective intimacy."[23] Or in Kafka's turn of phrase, Western Jews around 1900 "understood" more Yiddish than they could comfortably admit.[24]

III

Kafka also recorded the spectacle of watching a film (suggestively titled *Finally Alone*) which starred the German-Jewish stage actors, the Herrnfeld Brothers, as one of his most moving cinematic experiences.[25] Not surprisingly, most scholarly assessments of *fin-de-siècle* Jewish theater in Berlin have also focused on the "Herrnfeld Theater," established by Anton and David Herrnfeld in the final decade of the nineteenth century. The Herrnfeld brothers ultimately developed a performance style so unique that the phrase

"Herrnfeld Theater" became a stock expression. I will have more to say about the "Herrnfeld style" in what follows. For now, suffice it to note that the Herrnfelds were *the* standard for comparison when one attempts to gauge what was "too Jewish" in performance culture of the period. Whenever popular theater ventured into "too Jewish" territory in Imperial Berlin, it was likely that the Herrnfelds were involved.

As a result, the Jewish irony of the Herrnfeld style was frequently mis-understood by critics, Jewish and non-Jewish alike. Jewish ones in particular were keen to discern a "lack of aesthetic quality" in Herrnfeld performances. Such criticisms were directed at the brothers' use of Yiddish and slapstick physicality.[26] Others saw the phenomenon of *Mauscheln* (speaking German with a Yiddish accent) as sufficient evidence of an antisemitic propensity, fearing that any caricature would confirm antisemites' prejudices.[27] For what feels shameful does not always get a laugh. Yet audiences did not laugh *at* the Herrnfelds as much as *with* them. In turn, the Herrnfelds did not just parody Yiddish-inflected German (also called *jüdeln*), but also Viennese dialect, the Berlin idiom, and other regional variants of German. The ear-liest American vaudeville was also "dialect theater," directed at immigrant audiences, Jewish, Irish, and German alike.[28]

Suspicion of the Herrnfelds ultimately revealed as much about the alleging party as about the actual performance. Instead of appreciating the brothers' comic abilities, German-Jewish critics at the turn of the century objected that they were "too Jewish."[29] By the late 1920s, though, a major change was under way. Critics began to reassess the Herrnfelds. The positive spin brought together both the Liberal Jewish *C.V.-Zeitung* (the Anti-Defamation League publication of its day) and its Zionist rival, the *Jüdische Rundschau*. In time, reviewers for both organs came to acknowledge that it was unfair to accuse the Herrnfelds of "self-hatred," particularly after the rise of aggressively antisemitic discourse in mid-1920s Germany. Thus, the theater critic of the *Jüdische Rundschau* wrote: "I can't help it, and I may render myself a run-of-the-mill admirer of kitsch, a Jewish one, mainly for *Jewish* kitsch. But it [the Herrnfeld Theater] is great stuff."[30]

Looking back at the first year (1901) of *Ost und West*, Schach's critical prejudices proved trendsetting for the magazine, where an uncritical accep-tance of Eastern Jewish culture gradually took a back seat to Western Jewish middlebrow sensibilities. The magazine's drive to publish "legitimate" Jewish culture also applied to its status as a medium. Not to be perceived as a "low," cheap amusement, the magazine pretended to carry only high art and high culture. But from its inception, there were cracks and fissures in *Ost und West*'s project to make Yiddish "respectable."[31] In the same pages where one finds general bias against theater for the masses, the magazine gives voice to the diverse nature of Eastern Jewish dramatic culture offered in turn-of-the-century Berlin. In the August 1901 issue, a few months after Schach's fulminations, the audience at an evening of Yiddish theater is specifically described as "uniformly Jewish" and "serious." They "laugh hard" at the comic Yiddish *shtick* being performed, while managing to remain "classy" and "sophisticated."[32]

Who are these "uniformly Jewish" yet "restrained" theatergoers?[33] The author of the article elides the details. Extratextual evidence suggests that this audience consisted largely of working-class Eastern Jews at a performance in Berlin's disreputable *Scheunenviertel* (literally "barn quarter"), north of the Alexanderplatz.[34] (The Scheunenviertel also had one of Europe's highest densities of cinemas and carnivals.) In fact, around 1900, there were already at least two distinct Jewish theatergoing publics in Berlin. In the same August 1901 article of *Ost und West*, Winz and his co-workers were rendering Yiddish performance reputable for Western Jews, not for the East European Jews who had formed the original audiences for Yiddish theater in Berlin since the earliest documented performance of 1883.

Yet if one wishes to consider theater exclusively for Jews and written by Jews around 1900 in the German cultural sphere, one is compelled to look at popular Yiddish theater. Yiddish theater at the time was consciously *lowbrow*, closer to show business than high art. In fact, its earliest manifestations in late nineteenth-century Eastern Europe were entertainment oriented, encompassing operetta, musical comedy, and revue. Only after the encounter with Western theater practice did this melodramatic "kitsch" yield to modernist influences such as Naturalist and Expressionist drama, the emblematic example being S. Ansky's *The Dybbuk* (1919).

Music, song, and dance thus figured prominently in early Yiddish performances. In particular, traveling troupes copied Goldfaden's successful formula of mixing musical vaudeville with light comedy. Even though Yiddish theater since its beginnings involved varieté or revue, melodramatic "good kitsch" was imported from the West European stage in order to round out the repertoire. With time, educators and intellectuals called for a serious, "educational" Jewish theater, one that went beyond "making people laugh or cry."[35] Still, that "good" kitsch remained popular, even with Goldfaden, who himself had at first concurred with the reformers. Near the end of his career, he explained: "Laugh heartily if I amuse you with my jokes, while I, watching you, feel my heart crying. Then brothers, I'll give you a drama, a tragedy drawn from life, and you shall also cry – while my heart shall be glad.[36]

Critics of Yiddish theater, however, continued to be concerned that educational value be provided to its working-class audiences.[37] Not surprisingly, theater reform in this era paralleled developments in the nascent medium of cinema. The middle classes in Germany, like Kafka and others throughout the world, were lured by the spectacle of the silver screen. By 1910 or so, the larger project of acquiring respectability for the movies was complete, in both Europe and the United States. Even though many in Germany initially feared or rejected film as "low culture," studios and producers had set about to make the medium respectable. Through well-appointed moviehouses and middlebrow films, the new industry successfully attracted bourgeois viewers.[38]

At its zenith between the late nineteenth century and World War II, Yiddish theater could be found not only in Jewish Eastern Europe but also in Jewish neighborhoods in Berlin, Vienna, Prague, Paris, London, and New York City. From the start, Yiddish theater was very much an international theater. That *Berlin* Yiddish theater dates back to the year 1883 is no coincidence. The ban on Yiddish performances in Russia followed the assassination of Tsar Alexander II in 1881 and lasted until the 1905 Revolution, effectively shifting the locus of Yiddish theater toward Western Europe and the United States.

The upheavals in Russia brought half a million new Jewish immigrants to New York between 1905 and 1908. Once again, as in the first wave of the 1880s, many Yiddish theatergoers sought out lighter fare. As in Berlin, this kitsch was not always characterized as "bad," nor was it performed poorly. Some actor/producers, such as Jacob Adler (1855–1926), performed the newly emerging classics of the "higher" Yiddish theatrical repertoire, but Boris and Bessie Thomashefsky (the grandparents of conductor/composer Michael Tilson Thomas) succeeded in reading their New York audiences right. In rehabilitating the popular *kitsch* style, they made a significant profit off *shund* ("trash") theater. Many today still associate this style, often sentimental and larger-than-life, with the Yiddish stage.[39]

Shifting from weepy melodrama to wild Purimspiel, *shund* became a term of the trade. And the struggle between *shund* and *kunst* ("art") played itself out across the international Yiddish scene. The popular "Jüdische Bühne" in Vienna, for example, was "an entertainment theater, which knew its audience and its desires well."[40] Its fare consisted mainly of operetta, melodrama, and proto-musicals – not unlike the offerings in Prague to which Kafka was exposed. The productions were thus closer to vaudeville, i.e., brief comic *shticks* interrupted by short musical interludes and often based on hastily composed texts. As elsewhere, a movement developed in Vienna to reform the Jewish stage.[41] In Berlin, less populated by *Ostjuden*, the situation was not very different. At first, there was Quarg's Theater, also known as Quarg's Vaudeville, as well as Puhlmann's Varieté and the main competitor of the Herrnfelds, the Folies Caprice. Although their names and locations differed, each featured revue theater. The one-act plays, songs, comedy, and similar attractions made it relatively easy for traveling troupes from Eastern Europe to guest from time to time.

The origins of the Herrnfeld Theater also lay in such varieté, although not of the Yiddish type. Instead, the recipe for the Herrnfelds' remarkable success was a self-reflexive deployment of Jewish stereotypes. According to Peter Sprengel, a historian of Berlin theater, the Herrnfelds did not set out to ridicule or scorn things Jewish. Rather, they depicted Jewishness from a Jewish perspective, i.e., "with self-irony." The Herrnfelds practiced a form of "ethnic comedy" (*Ethno-Komik*), which emerged out of a "tension between caricature and realism."[42] The stereotypes that the brothers manipulated not surprisingly became a matter of concern for those struggling against anti-semitism. They feared that the Herrnfelds' performances could and would be instrumentalized by anti-Jewish forces.[43]

Other theater historians come to similar conclusions on matters of kitsch and stereotyping. Peter Jelavich, the expert on Berlin and Munich cabaret history, writes that the more he has examined the Herrnfeld productions and other forms of popular theater in Berlin that were sympathetic to Jews, the more he sees

> a pattern of placing stereotypes of Jews (speaking "Jargon") with other stereotyped minorities in Germany, e.g. Saxons, Bavarians, Bohemians, and Berliners. All of these groups had stereotyped images in popular comedies, and they all spoke with their "funny" accents, but they generally were good-natured stereotypes (though they made thin-skinned purists of those groups cringe in dismay). By adding Jews to that German "ethnic" mix on a popular comic stage, the Herrnfelds were trying to pass the somewhat condescending, but ultimately feel-good attitudes generated toward Saxons, Bavarians, etc. in such works onto Jews as well.[44]

In diagnosing this subgenre as kitsch, Jelavitch argues that "it was kitsch that generated good vibes, and that contributed to a popular image (though hardly a reality) of Jewish ethnicity." This type of ethnic comedy, multiply mediated as it was, is paralleled today by variety shows on television such as *Saturday Night Live*.[45]

IV

Historians of Western Europe and America have begun in recent years to probe the intersections of elite and popular culture after 1900. From the written word to visual art and the cinema, a war of taste was being waged. The drive to make "low" culture respectable was no less apparent in making Yiddish respectable. In fact, the *Kunst/Schund* distinction in German and German-Jewish milieux was precisely paralleled in the *kunst/shund* debates taking place in Yiddish-speaking Eastern Europe.

The rhetorical attacks on Yiddish popular theater involved the social realities of its not particularly *justes milieux*.[46] Until the rise of avant-garde drama after World War I, forever linked with S. Ansky (1863–1920) and the Vilna Troupe, the audience and appeal of Yiddish theater were overwhelmingly lower or working class. Winz (of *Ost und West*) was no doubt aware that the backers of the veritable Yiddish "Broadway" in Warsaw were "Yekl Shapshavitshes," i.e., underworld bosses. (Yekl Shapshavitsh, the protagonist of Asch's *God of Vengeance*, is a brothel-keeper.) That Jewish historiography, particular since the Holocaust, has insistently denied the existence of this theater *demi-monde* is equaled only by the denial of a Jewish criminal world in European history, which Gershom Scholem (1897–1982), in addition to his research on Jewish mysticism, considered a necessary pursuit.[47]

Kafka became acquainted with Yiddish theater in a rather tawdry Prague nightclub run by a brothel-keeper. Winz was also familiar with these "low" milieux and rumored to be associated with them.[48] In fact, the history of *his* backing of Yiddish theater in Germany is shot through with stereotypical rhetoric about that theater. It is in just such a framework that *Ost und West* was continually inventing ways to make Yiddish reputable. In addition to the venues in Berlin's Scheunenviertel that actually performed in Yiddish, there were of course rare adaptations of Yiddish drama in German translation, as in the 1907 performance of Sholem Asch's *God of Vengeance* at Max Reinhardt's *Kammerspiele*, probably the most prestigious theatrical venue in turn-of-the-century Berlin.[49]

On linguistic grounds alone, it would have been difficult for Western Jews to appreciate Yiddish-language drama. The case of Kafka is the exception that proves the rule.[50] But even those few bohemians willing to acquaint themselves with actual Yiddish performances, ten years prior to Kafka's fateful meeting with Jitzchak Löwy (1887–1942), were unlikely to have attended them. For theater in Berlin's *Scheunenviertel* was a highly regulated practice. So regulated that there were in all likelihood fewer than five performances per year until 1908. In fact, over seventy censors' copies have survived of plays by Goldfaden, Jacob Gordin (1853–1909), Joseph Lateiner (1853–1935), Sigmund Feinmann, and others. As theater historian Peter Sprengel concludes:

> The strict interpretation of individual statutes in the theater code by the authorized censors actually worked to block, in part to ban, a Jewish theater praxis whose authentic forms – vagabond theater, hybrids of musical and spoken theater, etc. – existed in an obvious tension with the binding regulations for theater performance in Prussia. And it is not unusual for one to get the impression that this objectively given conflict was exploited and exacerbated by the responsible officials with a certain subjective gratification.[51]

This understanding is borne out in censors' reports that Sprengel and others have uncovered in the archives of the Berlin police. Brief disdainful descriptions abound, ranging from "burlesque," "pornographic," and "corrupting" to "slapstick," "pedestrian," and "moronic." To be sure, all these epithets have a measure of truth: Berlin Yiddish theater *was* performed in infamous circumstances. After avant-garde Yiddish drama registered its first triumphs in post-1918 Germany, similar charges were made against the popular

German-Jewish stages, such as the Herrnfeld Theater. Writer Alfred Döblin thus proclaimed in 1921 that this type of theater, based on "self-prostituting, disgraceful pseudo-Jewish dialect" (*das sich selbst prostitutiernde unwürdige Gemauschel*), was hopefully at an end.[52]

The situation of Eastern Jewish actors in Germany was at best precarious, as was that of other non-citizens in Imperial Germany. Foreign performers not in possession of a permit or authorized to perform in public ran the risk of being deported. In addition, the earliest examples of Yiddish theater in Germany were viewed by the authorities as a threat, not only to the tax base but also to the "social order."[53] The broad administrative powers granted German civic officials did not have to be used, however. And yet Alexander Granach (1890–1941), the Galician Jewish immigrant who became a featured actor in Max Reinhardt's theater, spoke for many Eastern Jews in the Scheunenviertel when he *praised* the revolutionary tendencies of early Yiddish drama: "He [the playwright Gordin] was for the poor and against the rich. For the whores and against the fine ladies. For the orphans and the bastards and against those who'd achieved wedded security. He was also for me."[54]

This potential for social contestation may explain the five-year silence of *Ost und West* concerning Yiddish theater. In a December 1902 article – the only one to appear on the subject until 1907 – "A Jewish Stage in Galicia" is exalted. This Lemberg-based theater which influenced Granach to become an actor in the first place is praised for its directness and lack of (Western) sophistication. Its actors are further lauded as "simple children of nature," their style of theater comparing favorably with the popular *Schwänke* and *Possen* which constituted the broad mass of performances by the brothers Herrnfeld.[55]

Perhaps Schach's 1901 call for Jewish theaters to be granted concessions in neighborhoods heavily populated by Jews served ultimately to alert the Berlin police.[56] Winz's papers amply attest to the difficulties of being an Eastern Jewish entrepreneur in Germany in the first years of the century. And it was no accident that the earliest financial backers of *Ost und West* were (established) Western Jews such as Heinrich Meyer-Cohn, Otto Warburg, and Eduard Lachmann, for Prussian policy virtually required Russian (and other foreign) Jews to render themselves invisible.[57] Winz's magazine, then, was taking a risk in openly displaying Eastern Jewish leanings.

In 1906, however, *Ost und West* became a self-sustaining enterprise, completely and unquestionably under Winz's control. The Yiddish stage had by that time acquired a degree of respectability.[58] The Berlin police had also become more accustomed to it, and performances were becoming more frequent. In 1907, after Asch's *God of Vengeance* was performed in Berlin, *Ost und West* cautiously revived discussion of Yiddish drama, albeit in terms recalling Schach's Western-inflected discourse. Critic A. Coralnik, in a July 1907 review in the magazine, thus pans Asch and his Naturalist dramas, arguing that Asch is by no means the most talented of Jewish writers. His literary productions have soul, but not a deep and strong one; moods, but no toned-down, nuanced, fine ones; rhythm, but a monotonous one like the buzzing of a bee on a humid summer day; truths, but everyday, banal ones. There are realms of art that are inaccessible to him, corners of the soul that are invisible to him.[59]

Asch simply failed when compared with the recently canonized "classical" writers of Yiddish, Mendele Moykher-Sforim (1835–1917) and Isaac Leib Peretz, or with nineteenth-century German writers such as Christian Friedrich Hebbel (1813–63).

Samuel Meisels, the cultural editor of the Liberal-Jewish *Israelitisches Familienblatt*, also attacked Asch for his Naturalist aesthetic. In a contribution to *Ost und West*, he directed his fire first at Asch and then at Yiddish literature as a whole. For the Western Jewish Meisels, Yiddish literary history was "backward," paralyzed through "rhymed sermons," in desperate need of the Impressionist–Symbolist virtues of "emotional atmosphere, soul-release, [and] natural sentiment."[60] Yet, despite finding such fault, Meisels was himself actively engaged in translating and transmitting the culture of the *Ostjuden*, acknowledging the function of Yiddish theater as an educational institution for the Jewish masses. And it is worth recalling that his Jewish contemporaries in Eastern Europe shared similar biases concerning "high" and "low" culture.[61] To Sholem Asch, despite all the negative reviews of his work, it was worth raving that his dramas had been performed in Germany at all. According to the critic Samuel Niger, to succeed in Germany in those days was a form of *yikhes* (distinction).[62]

As German-Jewish writers such as Kafka, Kurt Pinthus (1886–1975), and Theodor Lessing (1872–1933) were gingerly beginning to write about the theater of Eastern Jews, the most popular venue for Yiddish performance in late Imperial Germany was actually the so-called "Young Jewish Evening" (*jungjüdischer Abend*) or "Evening of Songs" (*Liederabend*). Kafka himself organized one such evening, introducing the performances with a famous speech on the Yiddish language. From 1908 on, a considerable number of these pageant-like performances of music and poetry were produced by Winz and his *Ost und West* publishing firm.[63] The 1912 Berlin *Liederabend* was a hit by all accounts, prompting Winz to take his ensemble on two highly acclaimed tours of Germany, with concerts in Leipzig, Breslau, Munich, Nuremberg, Hamburg, Hannover, and elsewhere.[64]

A typical *Ost und West*-sponsored evening of "living literature and music" proved that recitation and folksong had more *cachet* than the pre-*Dybbuk* Yiddish theater. (The varieté phenomenon of the *Liederabende* has unexpectedly become the rage in post-1989 Berlin, albeit under the designation of "Klezmer evenings" of music and drama produced mainly for non-Jewish audiences.) Standards of the *Ost und West Liederabende* were performances of folksongs (from Winz's unrivaled personal collection) and readings from the translations of Yiddish prose published in *Ost und West*. These renderings into German, most of them by writer Theodor Zlocisti (1874–1943), were published in a two-volume edition by Winz in 1909. That book, *Aus einer stillen Welt* (*From a Serene World*) included works by Mendele, Peretz, Sholem Aleichem, Asch, Pinski, Reuben Braudes, Mordecai Spector, Abraham Reyzen, and Hersh David Nomberg.

The only other work that Winz published should come as no surprise: it was Ansky's *Dybbuk* in a 1920 translation prepared jointly by Winz and Arno Nadel (1878–1943). This first rendering of Ansky's drama into German had been commissioned by the author himself just prior to his death. It would exceed the scope of this chapter to chart Winz's further activities on behalf of the *Dybbuk*, which included an opera version for the German stage and an attempt at filming the drama with the Hebrew-language troupe, *Habima*.[65] Suffice it to say that he was very involved – legally as well as artistically.[66] The same was true in 1919 when Winz went to considerable expense to bring to Berlin the Alexander Azro/Sonja Alomis "spin-off" troupe of the Vilna art-theater. This was one of many guest engagements of Eastern Jews that Winz sponsored over the years, prompting writer and jurist Sammy Gronemann (1875–1952) to dub him "perhaps the most active friend and supporter of Jewish art in all areas."[67] For his initial involvement with Azro and Alomis, however, Winz lost more than 5000 (pre-inflation) *Marks*, even though he would later succeed in bringing the entire Vilna Troupe to Berlin for a two-year engagement.[68] Clearly, there was a great deal of money at stake in promoting the Yiddish theater in Weimar Germany. The competition was arguably fierce. Between 1919 and 1924, there were numerous agents and producers doing business in Berlin and at least twenty Yiddish publishing houses.[69]

That Yiddish theater by 1920 had become at least as respectable as it was profitable, in Germany and much of Central Europe, may to a large extent be on account of Winz's efforts to make Yiddish attractive. *Ost und West* and Winz's other enterprises contributed significantly to the cultural (and commercial) capital of Yiddish. Winz was, to be sure, a sufficiently clever cultural observer to wait for a critical mass before taking a risk himself. The timing was certainly right after 1906, at the latest after 1911, when the Berlin police stopped cracking down on Yiddish theater in the Scheunenviertel. After that, Winz was also safe to promote his *Liederabende* on a broad scale.

Because he lived in and "between" two cultures, Winz understood how to balance *Ost und West*'s advocacy of East European Jewish culture with the demands of its Western Jewish audiences. Although *Ost und West* was the first significant publication to bring together Western and Eastern Jewish intellectuals and artists, its accomplishments lie more in the realm of cultural transmission than in intellectual or artistic innovation. The same can be said of its depiction of Yiddish theater. Yiddish-language drama, music, and song appeared frequently in the magazine from its inception, but the treatment of these texts valorized more the middlebrow than anything avant-garde. As seen, the earliest arrival of Yiddish theater in Germany was not as dignified as it might appear in the "authoritative" versions that appeared in *Ost und West*.

What few people have acknowledged, however, is that, prior to Buber's translations – or better "rewritings" – of Hasidic tales, *Ost und West* was the largest transmitter of Eastern Jewish literature, art, and folklore to the Western Jewish public.[70] Besides acting as an editor and publisher, Winz was also a collector of Eastern Jewish art and music and a patron to those who produced it.[71] Besides earning money for Winz and Eastern Jewish artists, *Ost und West*'s practical functions included spotlighting relief efforts for Russian, Rumanian, and other Jews in need; the magazine was a leading publicity organ for Jewish philanthropy in Eastern Europe and elsewhere. Winz and his associates saw no contradiction in championing Eastern Jewish grass-roots initiatives while at the same time endorsing Western-based relief efforts.

Ost und West, though, did on occasion misrepresent features of Eastern Jewish culture. Some of the translations into German reveal a selective reinvention of "native" traditions. Yet even when they made mistakes, contributors to the magazine inspired imitators, such as Fritz Mordechai Kaufmann (1888–1921), the founder of *Die Freistatt* (Site of Freedom; Eschweiler, 1912–14). *Die Freistatt* was indebted to *Ost und West* for its early attempts to publicize Eastern Jewish culture, along with *Neue jüdische Monatshefte* (New Jewish Monthly; Berlin, 1916–24) and Buber's *Der Jude* (The Jew; Berlin, 1916–24).[72] Just how envious Buber was of Winz's success as a publicist can be seen in his 1903 sketch for *Der Jude*. This ambitious project, which he conceived along with Chaim Weizmann (1874–1952), Lilien, and Alfred Nossig (1864–1943) – whose wife later sued Winz for the rights to Ansky's *Dybbuk* – was intended to become a literary and cultural monthly similar to Winz's. Because of lack of funds and *Ost und West*'s greater appeal, *Der Jude* was shelved until 1916 when interest in East European Jewry was sufficient to warrant another major pan-Jewish journal. On balance, then, Winz and his magazine should be remembered for pioneering the advocacy of East European Jewry in the West long before the emergence during World War I of what Gershom Sholem dubbed the "cult of the *Ostjuden*."[73]

V

The members of the Bar-Kochba Society came because of the name of the drama and must have been disappointed. Knowing Bar-Kochba only from this drama, I wouldn't have named a society after him.

On the performance of Abraham Goldfaden's *Bar Kochba* on
November 4, 1911 in Café Savoy in Prague; Kafka, *Diaries*,
November 6, 1911[74]

When he proposed that his (then) fiancée Felice Bauer (1887–1960) stray from her upper-middle-class haunts in Berlin to catch a performance of his friend Jitzchak Löwy's troupe, Franz Kafka proved himself more ethnographically minded than critics of the culture industry.[75] His warning to Felice that the theater in question would most likely be "shabby" should not be misread: Kafka was neither a snob nor had he set foot in the Scheunenviertel at this time. Before he even lived in Berlin, Kafka grasped the cultural sociology of the Yiddish theater, as his lecture on Yiddish and his empathetic encounter with Löwy's troupe in Prague made clear.[76]

While Felice Bauer may not have acted upon Kafka's suggestion, she appears to have been a regular reader of *Ost und West*, bringing her (sometime) fiancé's attention to important reviews published there.[77] Indeed, Kafka may have had the magazine and Eastern Jewish culture in mind when formulating his thoughts on Christmas Day, 1911, in the famous fragment on the culture of "minor" nations:

> [T]he stimulating of minds, the integrated cohesion of national consciousness, often unrealized in public life and always verging on disintegration, the pride and support that a nation derives from a literature of its own in the face of hostile surroundings, this keeping of a diary by a nation which is something quite different from historiography and leads to more rapid (and yet always closely scrutinized) development, the elaborate spiritualization of a wide-ranging civic life, the immediately useful uniting of dissatisfied elements when carelessness can only do harm, the comprehensive organization of a people *that is created by the hustle and bustle of magazines* [...] – all these effects can be produced by a literature whose development is not unusually broad in scope but only seems so because it lacks notable talents.[78]

Since Kafka's reflections here, the field of Yiddish Studies has itself achieved *academic* respectability, however tenuous. Yet what may be needed today is a movement to unsettle matters, to render Yiddish, its theater, and its spectators a little *less* respectable. The present argument (if persuasive) will have begun to problematize the Jewish reception of Yiddish performance, not only in early twentieth-century Germany but also in current scholarship.

This chapter further begs the question of "the Jewish audience" and its practices as an interpretive community. While the circumstances of Yiddish theater in pre-Nazi Germany were infinitely more complex than can be reconstructed, its earliest Eastern Jewish participants, both on and off the stage, were quite sophisticated. Their agency and aptitude are verified in two very similar assessments by two very different Jewish theater mavens in Germany. Theodor Lessing, the liberal *yekke* publicist, concluded that "they're laughing at themselves in bitter seriousness."[79] Alexander Granach, the prototypical *Ostjude* in Germany, concurred: "We bitched mercilessly about the bad plays and the bad acting, but kept going back all the same."[80] What unites both interpreters, one Western and the other Eastern born, constitutes a lesson for us today about the complexities that attend the reception of both high and low culture.

The Yiddish theater that made such an impression on Kafka was laced with affectionate, even bittersweet irony. The tragicomic nostalgia for the *shtetl* evident in contemporary "klezmer culture" – in fact, the klezmer revival in post-Holocaust Berlin is now two decades old – corresponds to developments in the nineteenth-century Yiddish theater.[81] In retrospect, but without "backshadowing," we today might still respond to Yiddish popular performance with that combination of identification and distancing signified by irony. For irony's synthesis of critique and recovery presents a productively problematizing approach to German-Jewish culture in the wake of National Socialism and the Holocaust.

2

"*SCHLEMIEL*, SHLIMAZEL"

A proto-postcolonialist satire of "Jews," "Blacks," and "Germans"

I

To whom, then, did the Jews speak in that much talked about German-Jewish dialogue? They spoke to themselves, or rather, they *outshouted* one another.

> Gershom Scholem, "Against the Myth of the German-Jewish 'Dialogue,'" 1962[1]

Let the Arabs have Uganda.

> A Lubavitcher Hasid in Postville, Iowa, ca. 1994

In the first issue of the Zionist-sponsored *Der Schlemiel: Illustriertes jüdisches Witzblatt* [The Schlemiel: An Illustrated Journal of Jewish Humor] in 1903, a satirical column was introduced as a way of commenting on new Jewish nationalist controversies such as Great Britain's offer of territory in Uganda for a Jewish homeland.[2] Titled "Briefe aus Neu-Neuland" [Letters from New-Newland] – a pun on Theodor Herzl's controversial 1902 utopian work *Altneuland* [Old-New-Land] – this series of satires features a Ugandan chieftain named Mbwapwa Jumbo.[3] In his first correspondence with *Schlemiel*, accompanied by a portrait, this black-skinned "native" draws a perceptive analogy between the experiences of (East) European Jews and African-Americans:

> Lieber *Mister* Schlemiel! Als meine Landsleute hörten, daß man geht zu machen eine *immigration* von Jews in Uganda, da haben sich alle *nigger* gestellt an den Victoria Nyanza, und in ihrem Schmerz haben sie geweint ihre Tränen hinein in den See. Nur ich habe behalten meinen guten Mut. "Warum tut ihr heulen?" hab ich gefragt. "Die *jewish nation* wird sein freundlich zu euch; denn sie ist geworden gelyncht in Europa wie der arme *nigger* in Amerika. Das gleiche Schicksal bringt die Menschen einander nahe, und sie werden sehen auf euch wie Brüder.[4]

29

After drawing the analogy between "Blacks" and "Jews," Jumbo converts to Orthodox Judaism and Mizrachi Zionism. With time, he becomes an Eastern (African) Jew, speaking a German admixed with Yiddish (and some English) syntax and vocabulary.

When first reading Jumbo's "Letters from New-Newland," I focused on the ideological contradictions. On the one hand, the letters reflected the generally positive attitudes of *Schlemiel*'s editors *vis-à-vis* colonized, Yiddish-speaking Jews of East European culture (referred to as "Eastern Jews" or *Ostjuden* in this book).[5] On the other hand, the letters repeated stereotypes of such Jews and caricatures of Black Africans becoming "wanna-be" *Ostjuden*. Resolving this contradiction seemed easy enough from the standpoint of ideology critique: it was "clearly" a discrepancy central to debates in turn-of-the-century Europe (especially Germany) regarding the status and nature of Jews, a discrepancy reflected in any number of discourses, and thus in *Schlemiel*.[6]

Yet, upon closer analysis, it became clear to me that the objective of the Western-born (but Eastern-oriented) Jews behind "Jumbo's letters" was to interrelate "Jews" and "Blacks" from an anti-colonialist perspective. In doing so, *Schlemiel*'s editors wished to attract a Westernized, acculturated Jewish audience to an agenda of public, "open" Jewishness, a type of Cultural Zionism (influenced in part by Ahad Ha'am). In the "Letters from New-Newland," *Westjuden* were newly enjoined to become "culturally" or "ethnically" Jewish.[7] At this moment, Jewish nationalism was still evolving, and might have taken a diverging path.

In attempting to legitimize and draw upon the culture and comic traditions of East European Jewry, *Schlemiel* had to overcome the negative perception of such Jews by many Western Jews (and non-Jews) since the Enlightenment. Nowadays, we would term the journal's agenda "postcolonial critique." But whereas performances by the colonized "of color" are well-known to American academics, those of the early colonized Jews of Europe have been overlooked.[8] John Efron, in *Defenders of the Race: Jewish Doctors and Race Science in Fin-de-Siècle Europe*, has examined Jewish nationalist scientists around 1900. He concludes that "[t]o accept the proposition that historically the Jews were involved in a colonial relationship with Christian Europe is to also recognize that the labors of Jewish [defenders of the race] were an attempt at reversing the European gaze."[9] There was, therefore, a small but significant difference between "German Orientalism" and its European Jewish variant. Taking the lead from Efron, "the categories of 'empire' and 'colonized' need to be expanded to include groups such as Jews, who do not fit neatly into the traditional paradigm of empire as that term is understood by anthropologists and historians."[10]

Schlemiel's political project, to extend Judith Butler's analysis of the constructed subject in *Gender Trouble* and *Bodies That Matter*, consisted not so much in overthrowing paradigms of race as in *deconstructing* the compulsory racialized "matrix" that supports such paradigms. In countering normative heterosexism, Butler proposes that we theorize fissures, interpreting texts for the ways they reflect and resist the pressures of signifying within the terms imposed by a gendered matrix. The early Zionist project, although it sought to reverse Jewish "assimilation" in Western and Central Europe, was similarly full of "racialized" fissures. These cracks in the ethnic–nationalist matrix were, we shall see, truly "schlemielist" moments, ripe for "resignification."

And it is precisely in *Schlemiel*'s "cracks" (if you'll pardon the pun) that a comedy of colonialism takes place. Zionism, in its initial "political" and "cultural" manifestations, contested existing Jewish political and cultural discourses. Indeed, it was its revolutionary potential of Jewish nationalism that alarmed both the Jewish Orthodox opponents of Zionism and Zionism's Mizrachi apologists. *Schlemiel* is thus historically situated at a cusp in the development of Zionist discourse. Its existence and resonance suggest that it provided a space for a Jewish satire of colonialism. The Jew in *Schlemiel*, by the close of Jumbo's missives from Uganda, is rendered a postcolonial subject, *avant la lettre*. Indeed, the final "Letter from Africa" renders the entire series a polemic against antisemitic colonizers. What is more, this tribute to Jewish proto-postcolonialism emerged ten years prior to the Balfour Declaration of 1917.

The stepchild of Lord Balfour and early Zionism, the modern state of Israel, has been tainted by association with the (West) European colonialist project, an association made most urgently since the 1967 occupation of the West Bank and Gaza. Yet the only similarity that Jumbo's story shares with anti-Zionist discourse today is its projection of European social contestations onto Africa. For the "Letters from New-Newland" operate not only as a Jewish internal satire of assimilation (or "self-colonization") based on a redeployed colonial stereotype of "Blacks." Nor are they merely a satire of early political Zionism taken to an extreme for Westernized, Germanophone Jews. Rather, the colonized Jew is at the center of *Schlemiel*.

II

Implicit in the idea of the Jew as a "proto-postcolonial" subject is the Jew's performativity as a "schlemiel." Although *schlemiel* and its companion term *schlimazel* were adopted into American vernacular only after *Schlemiel* and after the Holocaust, they were well-known in (Eastern) European Jewish discourse prior to the magazine. It was thus clear to readers of *Der Schlemiel* that the schlemiel could be cast as a colonizer for whom all good intentions fail. For those unfamiliar with the terms: when a *schlimazel* drops a piece of buttered toast, it always lands buttered side down; when a *schlemiel* drops the piece of toast, *both* sides have likely been buttered.

Schlemiel's implicit "schlemielism" has a historical *longue durée*. According to Daniel Boyarin, the Jew has been (internally) valorized at least since the destruction of the Second Temple (in 70 C.E.) for his passivity, non-violence, and the gendered stereotype of "femininity" subtending those terms. Put differently, the "rabbinic Jew" in Western Christian civilization would rather be a "schlimazel" than a "schlemiel." The ethnic particularism preferred by rabbinic civilization only becomes a menace when combined with dominion over others. That is, over *other* "Others." One might say that the would-be Jewish colonizer, as caricatured in *Schlemiel*, is precisely such a schlemiel.

Taking this paradigm of Jewish powerlessness one step further: during the seventeen centuries between the Mishnah and the modern advent of Zionism, the rabbis taught that Jewish survival need not lead to a resort to political violence. The violent exercise of power was considered un-Jewish, an exhibiting of insolent pride that could only bring catastrophe. As David Biale explains in *Power and Powerlessness in Jewish History*: "The rabbis built a much more durable political system than had any of the earlier leaders, whether tribal elders, kings, or priests, who were only partially successful in confronting an imperial world and in maintaining some partial semblance of Jewish sovereignty."[11] Hannah Arendt, in her 1944 essay "The Jew as Pariah," recognized a post-Biblical advocate of such non-colonizing Jews. In his poem "Princess Sabbath" (1851), that advocate, Heinrich Heine, claimed an apocryphal descent for poets from "Herr Schlemihl ben Zurishaddai" – a name derived from the leader of the tribe of Simeon. Arendt explained:

> Heine relates the name to the word *schlemihl* by the humorous supposition that by standing too close to his brother chieftain Zimri he got himself killed accidentally when the latter was beheaded by the priest Phinehas for dallying with a Midianite woman (cf. Numbers 25: 6–15). But if they may claim Shelumiel as their ancestor, they must also claim Phinehas – the ruthless Phinehas whose "spear is with us,/And above our heads unpausing/We can hear its fatal whizzing/And the noblest hearts it pierces." History preserves to us no "deeds heroic" of those "noblest hearts." All we know is that – they were *schlemihls*.[12]

It is relevant to note that "Phinehas" [*sic*] is originally an Egyptian, and not a Hebrew, name. More importantly, his actions would have qualified as "violent" by the standards of the Talmudic sages.

Although not acquired with violence, Uganda was clearly an awkward site in 1903 for Jewish national survival. Herzl, in perhaps *his* most "schlemie-list" moment ever, put forth the Uganda plan nonetheless. In attempting to persuade some Cultural Zionists (the Democratic Faction) and more Religious Zionists (the Mizrachi Faction) to support Uganda as a temporary shelter (*Nachtasyl*) at the Sixth Zionist Congress, Herzl had been motivated by the failure of his diplomatic efforts as well as the deteriorating situation of Russian Jewry on the eve of the 1905 revolution. What was conceived as a way-station for Russian Jewish "schlimazels" promptly became the occasion for a "schlemielist" political (and moral) scandal among early Jewish nationalists. Herzl, in fact, may have recognized his own "schlemielism" while performing (i.e., reading out loud) a *Schlemiel* parody on the Uganda plan for friends in April 1904.[13] It is altogether possible that he was reading a contribution in a recent issue of the journal. There, in the fictitious minutes from a night session of a Zionist Congress, delegates are said to call for the establishment of a "Central Office for Schlemiel Activities" (*Zentrale für Schlemieligkeiten*).[14]

In retrospect, the Zionist flirtation with Uganda bears out Daniel and Jonathan Boyarin's claim that rabbinic Judaism's

> particular discourse of ethnocentricity is ethically appropriate only when the cultural identity is an embattled (or, at any rate, non-hegemonic) minority....Given the choice between an ethnocentricity that would not seek domination over others and a seeking of political domination that would necessarily have led either to a dilution of distinctiveness, tribal warfare, or fascism, the Rabbis chose ethnocentricity.[15]

Few religious Jews adhered to the subversion of Rabbinic Judaism that Zionism represented at this time. Among them were the Mizrachi Zionists, the object of much caricature in *Schlemiel*.

The analysis I have outlined explains in part why Jumbo – the ex-chieftain and now Jewish-leader – becomes an adherent of Mizrachi Zionism. In its openness towards the Enlightenment (*Haskalah* in Hebrew) and modern nationalism, this first Religious Zionist party was an unprecedented response to Orthodox anti-Zionists in late nineteenth-century Eastern Europe. When the "Letters from New-Newland" appeared, Mizrachi was already an internal political force to reckon with. In fact, one-third of the delegates at the Sixth Zionist Congress were Mizrachi – by far the largest faction present. During the Uganda controversy and in the last two years of his life, Herzl paid more attention to this bloc than to any other within the official Zionist organization, even funding it out of his own pocket or from the (dwindling) resources of the *Aktionskomitee*.[16] Mizrachi Zionists repaid him by becoming his most loyal allies. Going beyond conventional discipline in coalitions, their obedience was conspicuous.[17] And that rendered them, at least for the satirists of *Schlemiel*, ripe for ridicule.

III

Before proceeding further, it is helpful to situate *Schlemiel*'s satire in turn-of-the-century cultural discourse. When Emperor Wilhelm II acceded to the throne in 1888, the German *Kaiserreich* had "a more numerous and wider range of satirical journals than any other European country."[18] From today's vantage point, it is striking how sharply imperial policies – and Wilhelm II himself – were the butt of critique in popular publications such as *Simplicissimus, Kladderadatsch, Lustige Blätter*, and *Der wahre Jacob*. The jurisdictional flexibility that had previously permitted any local official in Germany to bring charges against an editor or cartoonist was abolished in 1900.

It might also help to draw an analogy with the contrasting styles of American popular humor in the same time-frame. A restrained Victorian comic sensibility termed "refined humor" or "thoughtful laughter" was being challenged by a more raucous, immediate form. In Europe as well as in the United States, this so-called "new humor," previously restricted to clubs and cafés, achieved wider dissemination after the 1880s. Joke books, humor magazines, newspaper parodies, and variety theater were soon to become staples of the European scene. As one might expect, the performance conventions and stock characters that defined these genres coexisted uncomfortably *vis-à-vis* the avant-garde.

The task of marketing this new humor under the mantle of Jewish nationalism was well-suited to Leo Winz (1876–1952), the transplanted Ukrainian Jew and public relations adept who founded *Schlemiel* as well as *Ost und West: Illustrierte Monatsschrift für modernes Judentum* (Berlin: 1901–23).[19] (On *Ost und West* [East and West], see Chapter 1.) Keenly aware of the need to conduct audience research in order to realize higher advertising revenues, Winz was a savvy entrepreneur and sponsor of the arts, music, boxing, and film. Years later, Winz would claim in his memoirs that *Schlemiel* was a successful weapon in the fight against both assimilation and antisemitism. Like other contemporaries, he saw no apparent contradiction here: ridiculing assimilated Jews would not *ipso facto* lead to antisemitism. On more than one occasion, Winz (a self-identified "Zionist") poked fun at Theodor Herzl, an exemplar of the "assimilated Jew" (even for some "Zionists"). But, as if to prove that it takes one to know one, Herzl approved implicitly of such tactics. He thus counseled the editors of the Zionist organization's newspaper *Die Welt* that "the assimilated provide such an ample target for humorous depiction that you won't ever lack for material."[20]

Although Herzl and Winz appeared to have a healthy sense of humor, their relationship was anything but jovial. When the Zionist leadership decided to take over *Schlemiel* after Winz could no longer afford to produce it, Winz sued to protect what he saw as his intellectual property. *Schlemiel* returned in the fall of 1903 under the editorship of its contributors Max Jungmann (1875–1970) and Sammy Gronemann (1879–1952). Both were Zionist insiders and each had a keen sense for satire. The new editors changed one letter in the title – from *Schlemihl* with "ihl" to *Schlemiel* with "iel" – and outdid Winz by making fun of the pending court case. No one, in fact, was exempt from ridicule in *Schlemiel*, least of all the "renowned Jewish artists and writers" who contributed to it.[21]

Although its circulation was perhaps no more than 5,000, *Schlemiel* was edited by and directed toward a number of influential German-reading Jews. Assuming that individual issues were passed along, actual distribution may have been as high as 20,000. This constituted a significant portion of Jewish Central Europe and was thus at least comparable to the audience saturation (of German-speaking Jews and non-Jews) achieved by *Simplicissimus* (at 85,000 sales per month) or *Der wahre Jacob* (ca. 300,000 subscribers in 1911) in the same period.[22] The Zionist leadership recognized *Schlemiel*'s potential for propaganda and agitation early on. A seasoned journalist, Herzl himself advised writing for a larger audience and adding better illustrations. Despite its harsh critiques of the Zionist leadership, the magazine was among Herzl's favorite reading, even on his deathbed.[23] Indeed, the popular (but non-Zionist) *Israelitisches Familienblatt* made repeated bids to appropriate *Der Schlemiel*, promising to make it into an even more "effectual force in the Jewish Renaissance."[24] (For more on the *Israelitisches Familienblatt* [Israelite Family Journal], see Chapter 5.)

Perhaps the most talented Jewish nationalist humorist of his day, Jungmann is the likely suspect for (main) author of the "Letters from New-Newland." Born in Schildberg, Posen, in 1875, he was no stranger to *Ostjuden* and used promotional methods similar to his good friend Winz's to re-valuate Eastern Jewry's status in internal Jewish debates. He, along with Gronemann, further perfected these techniques as one of Zionism's leading "spin doctors." In fact, two years after the Uganda debacle, Gronemann would specifically instruct delegates at the Seventh Zionist Congress to make greater use of visual images and symbols in order to increase the organization's following.

The first letter from Uganda (cited above) bears out Jungmann's and Gronemann's concern for making Zionism and Zionist humor accessible. Jumbo and his *landslayt* (countrymen) convert to the Jewish religion, promising to give up pork in favor of noodle pudding, chopped liver, and Sabbath stew (*tcholent*). Yet when their new Mizrachi Zionist brothers chant "Afrika für die Schwarzen!" [Africa for the Blacks], they are not preaching black-Atlantic or pan-African nationalism. Rather, they are referring to themselves. For they too are "die Schwarzen" insofar as they characteristically dressed in black in their indigenous Eastern European milieu. Jumbo closes his first epistolary performance as follows:

> Denn wie Sie sehen auf dem Photo ich schicke Ihnen, bin ich selbst geworden ein *member* von der orthodoxen *Misrach-society*. Einer hat schon gemacht den Witz und hat gesagt, daß ich darstelle einen Schornsteinfeger unter den Negern.[25]

Performing is thematized here – by a Black African portrayed in what might be called "Jewface." (Editor Jungmann, at a dance ball sponsored by the *Schlemiel*, once appeared costumed – and in character – as Jumbo.)[26] For in the illustration of Jumbo that accompanies each letter, we see a black man – but not a Sambo caricature – dressed in a caftan, a yarmulke on his head, and *peyes* (forelocks) adorning his face. He is also marked by an umbrella, that most curious icon of nineteenth-century Englishmen and Jews.

Much of the comic invective of these letters, however, also targets assimilated (or assimilating) Jews typified by the Berlin-based Jewish Reform movement. Such centrifugal satire was achieved by stereotyping and marginalizing a small group within German Jewry, the least observant movement of those days. The "Letters from New-Newland" are replete with references to highly assimilated Jews, and are regularly juxtaposed with cartoons such as "Our Future Lies on the Water." There, a figure, dressed in Reform rabbinical garb, teeters on a tightrope over a swimming pool designated as "Baptismal Water" while a spectator declares: "Oh God! Oh God! I'm always scared he's going to fall in."[27]

The fourth letter of the series has Jumbo selected to be the Ugandan ambassador to Russia.[28] Unless he converts to Christianity, however, he will not be permitted to enter St. Petersburg and fulfill the terms of his appointment. As he is reluctant to be baptized (being now "firmly rooted" in Judaism), it is suggested that he first go to Berlin, where he can prepare himself for baptism through "warm-up exercises" in the "Reform congregation." Arguably the most hilarious "Brief aus Neu-Neuland" (installment five) describes how Reform Jews in Uganda introduce dancing into their Sabbath worship in an attempt to preclude the natives from "becoming antisemites."[29]

Caveat lector: what may offend political correctness today has to be historicized and contextualized. For what was most unsettling around 1900 was the anti-colonialist discourse of the "Letters from New-Newland." Indeed, ex-chieftain Jumbo's epistolary novel is to be read as an anti-colonialist *Bildungsroman* in which the African "native" is transformed into a "Jew." In the episodes following his conversion by colonializing Mizrachi "schlemiels," he is taught Yiddish, he is drawn into a (Ugandan-based) movement to settle Palestine, and then forced to emigrate to Galveston, Texas, where he nearly falls victim to a pogrom. In this parody, Jumbo is thus changed from a presumably "tough" African warrior into a "cowardly," effeminized, and ultimately colonized Jew.

Even though this type of humor might appear to appeal to male readers, in *Schlemiel*, it gestures toward the anti-militaristic, anti-athletic traditions of (post-Rabbinic) East European Jewry. Whereas the ideal of manliness inherent in the ideal of Western (Christian) respectability served to brand Eastern Jews as "uncivilized," *Ostjuden* themselves appeared undaunted by the charge.[30] From Lithuania to Bessarabia, Eastern Jews did not exactly share non-Jewish body ideals. While Jewish thinkers in Western Europe distanced themselves more and more from physical stereotypes of Eastern Jews, the thin, pale Jewish scholar was considered to be the epitome of male beauty in Ashkenazic milieus. Whereas westernized Jews by the end of the nineteenth century idealized martial culture, physical prowess, and strong nerves, many Eastern Jews still subscribed to (post-Rabbinic) ideals of male gentleness, physical restraint, and non-violence. Jumbo eventually becomes so "Jewish" that, when he is designated ambassador to Russia, he reacts to the news as follows:

> Vor Schreck mein schwarzes Gesicht war bleich wie Kreide, sodaß Chaskel hat genommen meine Hände und gefragt: "Mister Jumbo, Sie sind plötzlich so weiß geworden – sind Sie an Assimilant?" Ich aber bin gefallen ihm um den langen Hals und hab gejammert und geschrien: "Wie soll ich verlassen meine geliebte Heimat? Wie soll ich gehen zu *a people* von lauter Gaslonim, wo man wird morden mich, wenn man sieht, daß ich bin ein Jude!"[31]

In the conclusion to his adventures, set in Texas, Jumbo resolves to return with his Mizrachi brethren to his indigenous Uganda. The final "Letter from New-Newland" coincides not only with *Schlemiel*'s last regular issue (Purim [festival] 1907) and the British withdrawal of the Uganda offer, but also with the full revelation of the effects of German colonialism on the "dark continent." Between 1904 and 1907, an estimated 100,000 Herero were slaughtered in German South-West Africa (now Namibia) while resisting their occupiers' plans for their lands and resources. And in German East Africa (now Tanzania), an estimated 120,000 Africans were killed under similar circumstances. It was none other than Hannah Arendt (in her *Origins of Totalitarianism*) who first surmised a link between these massacres and the Holocaust.[32]

In *Schlemiel*, however, these murderous campaigns became the stuff of satire, as was often the case in East European Jewish history (in general) and the folklore of the schlemiel (in particular).[33] In this final letter from New-Newland, the German empire and its symbols are repeatedly attacked:

> [U]nd wie wir gingen durch die Strassen, links ich, in der Mitte der weisse Chaskel und rechts der rote Indianer, wir haben ausgesehen wie eine deutsche Flagge.

Black, white, and red: here the German imperial flag is reified with *and* through the bodies of Jew, African, and Native American. This new homology now becomes (proto-)postcolonial humor and a parody of Territorialist Jewry's "Galveston Plan." For what was at first a splinter movement within Zionism that favored the Uganda Plan, the Jewish Territorial Organization

(ITO) worked to establish Jewish settlements outside of Palestine between 1907 and 1917. It may be no coincidence that Israel Zangwill, the British Zionist leader of the Territorialist faction, had originally congratulated Jungmann on the title for the journal, noting that "we all are Schlemiels."[34]

After the three get beaten up in the Galveston episode, it is not Jumbo, but his light-skinned sidekick, Chaskel the Scribe, who yearns for Uganda. "MEIN freies Land," writes Jumbo and continues: "Bei uns und in ganz Afrika, wie Dir kann bestätigen die deutsche Kolonialverwaltung, heisst das Sprichwort: 'Willst mein Kusinchen sein? Sonst schlag' ich dir den Schädel ein.'"[35] Here, the inglorious recipient of aggressive, violent German imperialism is marked as a diminutivized linguistic female (*Kusine*). This final suggestion that Jumbo and his cohort are inadequately masculine is further associated with circumcision. In the illustrated salute to Jumbo and his buddy Chaskel that closes the "Letters from New-Newland," both are physically stripped of their clothing. Though not sexually explicit, the drawing (a send-up of a famous lithograph by the Zionist artist E. M. Lilien) intimates their exposure as circumcised *Ostjude* and circumcised *Afrikajude*. Even if Jumbo can now fulfill his explicit wish to "drop out of" (*austreten*) the Jewish "race" (*Rasse*), he cannot depart from the Jewish community of faith, having chosen *brit milah* (the "covenant" of circumcision).

IV

We have seen that it is something of a different order when stereotypes of East European Jews are taken and grafted onto representations of African Blacks in the context of a satire publication, especially one such as *Schlemiel*, intended exclusively for a Jewish audience. As folklorist Eliott Oring sees it, humor depends upon the listener's perception of an "appropriate incongruity" – a longstanding paradigm in humor research and theory.[36] In other words, both the "appropriateness" but "incongruity" of Eastern Jews trying to impose their culture onto black Africans should – among other possibilities – result in humor. To get the joke, though, the listener also has to attend to

> the context of rules, conventions, and understandings of the culture
> in which humor is communicated; the context of the humorous
> repertoire of which a joke is but a single element; the context of the
> situation and interaction in which it is expressed; [and] the context
> of the life of the individual who performs and enjoys it.[37]

Oring's essay is serious, and so is its implication for the present study, namely that the editors and contributors to *Schlemiel* stereotyped Africans and Jews in order to promote – but also to deconstruct – identity politics and other essentialisms. This should come as no great revelation: stereotypes were a time-tested, effective means of attracting Jewish audiences in Western Europe to Jewish nationalism. Negative stereotyping in particular was an alternative to dry idealized models of ethnic Jewishness. As Alan Dundes, the premier folklorist of the last generation, maintained: "Despite the clearcut pejorative cast of [...] ethnic slurs, it is important to realize that most of the slurs are told and *enjoyed* by members of the group concerned."[38] Here, they have a constitutive function, and are thus "part of ethnic identity."[39]

To be sure, stereotypes are forms of bias that can be used to slander and wound. But as they can be understood in terms of cognitive psychology as both contingent and necessary, stereotypes can also serve as a means of unsettling received images. In fact, no discussion of "Jews," "Blacks," and "Germans" would be complete without reference to the conscious inversions of Oskar Panizza's "The Operated Jew" (1893), Salomo Friedlaender's "The Operated Goy" (1922), and Edgar Hilsenrath's *The Nazi and the Barber* (1970). Especially the last two by "Jewish Germans" raise ethnic humor to the level of critical theory. In concluding his analysis of these three grotesque satirists, Jack Zipes claims that "[u]ntil the subversion is complete, that is, until we learn to resist domination through empathy and laughter, [as] Friedlaender suggests, we shall never know ourselves."[40]

For all its proto-postcolonial zeal, then, *Schlemiel* also reveled in self-effacement, and this practice was in contrast to other for-profit satire publications. Whereas the better known *Simplicissimus* purveyed high-end humor in Wilhelmine Germany, practically no one – from the Central Association of German Citizens of the Jewish Faith to hard-core Political or Cultural Zionists – was spared the parodic force of *Schlemiel*. Fairness in stereotyping was simply part of *Schlemiel*'s anti-heroic legitimation.

Yet despite the large bodies of research on humor and stereotyping, the relationship between the two has received less attention. Instead of employing value-laden categories such as "pathological" and "non-pathological," we are better served by a value-neutral approach that analyzes how effectively stereotypes are presented to specific social and cultural groups. By accounting for discursive context and mode of address, such an analysis also acknowledges that stereotypes are protean, that is "mutable and constantly shifting."[41] It is this inherent instability of stereotypes that enabled the image-makers behind *Schlemiel* to appeal to different markets and different senses of humor. The present study therefore affirms that stereotypes of the Jew, not to speak of the schlemiel, differ from culture to culture, institution to institution, and market to market.

Unfortunately, the idea that *German* Jews were lacking in humor still abides in the stereotype of the *yekke* (also spelled *Jekke*). While *yekke* first became a term of derision among Jews in 1930s Palestine, the stereotype has its origins in nineteenth-century Eastern Europe in Yiddish satires of the *daytsh* (Yiddish for "German Jew"). Yet *Schlemiel* and other evidence suggest that German Jews, even the few who were party Zionists, did not eschew popular entertainment despite the prevalence of "German" values in the German-Jewish propertied and educated middle classes. The final legacy of *Schlemiel* may be to remember that the term *Yekke* is etymologically related to *Jeck*, dialect for *Geck* (*fop* or *clown*) and cognate to *joker*. I am thus offering something along the lines of Philip Roth's Alexander Portnoy, who in the late 1960s endeavored to "put the *id* back in the *yid*." For the period around 1900, I propose no less than putting the *Jeck* back in the *Yekke*.

Doing so is not intended as a substitute agenda for "coming to terms with" the Holocaust. Further, there is no reason for German Jews, nor for other "Germans" and "Jews," to be laughing about racism or colonialism. And yet, on the (very famous) other hand: if *lakhn iz gezunt* (Yiddish: "laughter is healthy"), why can't there be *Heilen durch Humor* (German: "healing through humor")? By the same token, literary and cultural post-colonial criticism has been marked by a restraint verging on *reverence vis-à-vis* the wider significance and functions of laughter.[42] For if "oppressed people tend to be witty" (Saul Bellow), is it not also true that they prefer to take the first shot, making jokes about *themselves*? Among those who recognize Jewish self-irony to be a form of self-preservation is postcolonial theorist Homi Bhabha, who writes that

> [t]hrough the very performance of the self-critical joke-work there *emerges* a structure of identification – what Freud calls "the sub-jective determination of the joke-work" – that provides a way for minority communities to confront and regulate the abuse that comes from outside or the criticisms that emerge inwardly, from within the community itself.[43]

As Carl Hill notes in the conclusion to his book on Freud's diagnoses of "Jewish jokes": "*Witz* [is] poised on a cusp between utopia and apocalypse" (p. 230).[44] We today who write about the intersections of imperialism and mass culture may still respond to popular performance with that unsettling combination of distanciation and identification signified by the term "irony." Now, as nearly a century earlier, an ironic (and self-ironizing) historiography, one that integrates loss and rehabilitation, represents an alternative approach to the study of German-speaking Jewry and its cultural productions.

3

A GERMAN-JEWISH HERMAPHRODITE

Or what sexology contributed to B'nai B'rith

"I was born as a boy, raised as a girl."[1] That is the self-description of Karl M. Baer, "M" for "Martha," taken from his autobiographical narrative as a person born with stunted male genitalia in late nineteenth-century Germany. Misclassified at birth in 1885 by a small town doctor, Karl was brought up as a girl despite the signs that he looked and felt like a boy. In 1907, at the age of twenty-two, Baer legally assumed a masculine identity, a self-revision confirmed by the famous sexologist Magnus Hirschfeld who diagnosed Baer as a "pseudo-hermaphrodite." In the same year, Baer published a memoir under the genial pseudonym of "N. O. Body." *Aus eines Mannes Mädchenjahren* (From a Man's Girl Years – henceforth referred to as "Girl Years") went through at least six printings within the next two years, and served as the title for two feature films (1912 and 1919) loosely based on the story.[2]

A recent reprint, edited with a long essay by Hermann Simon, has brought the memoir renewed and deserved attention. Simon's essay, "Who was N. O. Body?", the result of twenty years of painstaking research, fills in most of the historical gaps. In particular, it reveals that N. O. Body was Karl Baer, and that Karl Baer was a Jew. After his becoming legally a man in 1907, Baer served as the director of the B'nai B'rith Lodges of Berlin, a Jewish social and welfare organization for men and women. Baer was by all accounts a gifted and model Jewish functionary. In September 1938, he immigrated to Palestine. Yet despite his importance in Weimar Jewish cultural life, Karl Baer had once been the same legal person – that is occupied the same body – as Martha Baer, a highly accomplished journalist, orator, social worker, feminist, and Zionist. All this transpired before the twenty-two-year-old Martha decided to affect a masculine persona and marry her female lover.

This chapter examines Jewish gender and sexuality as "entertainment" in a bestselling memoir that reveals how the popular concept of "self-hatred" functioned a century ago: as a rhetorical phenomenon, a trope that appealed to a (Jewish) middle-class readership. *From a Man's Girl Years* is the product of a complicated dialectic between the textual and the social, which compels a reassessment of German-Jewish history and memory.

I

Martha Baer's career paralleled that of her contemporary, Bertha Pappenheim, the founder of the League of Jewish Women (*Jüdischer Frauenbund*) established in 1908. Pappenheim is better known to posterity as Josef Breuer's patient "Anna O," who dubbed Breuer's proto-psychoanalytic treatment the "talking cure." In the guise of Martha, Karl Baer too had been a Jewish female activist, a leading figure in the struggle against "the white slave trade" (i.e., the prostitution) of East European Jewish women. Between 1904 and 1906, Baer worked tirelessly in Galicia and the Bukovina to uplift Eastern Jewish women socially and economically, leading efforts to organize working women by establishing literacy classes, employment bureaus, professional training, day care, and schools.[3] Although a Western Jew, Baer learned Yiddish and studied Polish, eventually falling in love with a Jewish woman from Czernowitz. Owing in part to that woman's difficult divorce, the two had contemplated suicide before Martha consulted the famous Dr. Hirschfeld, who then operated on her to correct her putative anatomical "deficiency." The two lovers thus could marry under the law; however, none of Karl Baer's three marriages produced children.[4]

In *Girl Years*, the twenty-two-year-old narrator reveals the ups and downs of a life characterized by mistaken identities, a situation exacerbated by the narrow-mindedness of town life in central western Germany at the close of the nineteenth century. On the surface, the memoir would seem to be a classic example of gender, sexual, and ethnic "self-hatred."[5] N. O. Body, the first-person narrator, hides or represses most traces of Karl Baer's Jewishness, his femininity, and any possible gay or lesbian desire.[6] Yet, when viewed more critically, the alteration of certain facts, a strategy designed to protect Baer and his loved ones, is much more a pragmatic decision than it is evidence of shame and embarrassment. Rather, the memoir tacitly challenges the idea that its author was "self-hating," that is, pathologically split and psychologically overdetermined. Whereas Baer may have at times experienced confusion or "gender ambivalence," the preponderance of evidence points to an incredible resilience in living out multiple roles – gender, ethnic, class, and so forth. Baer's resulting personality, then, need not be viewed negatively as the inevitable result of internalized anti-feminism, antisemitism or homophobia.

Instead, Baer's narrative shows how the popular concept of "self-hatred" may function at times as a rhetorical conceit, a meta-psychological trope that has to be contextualized historically. This trope, in the case of the N. O. Body memoir, was designed to appeal to large middle-class audiences favoring cheap entertainments and sensationalistic books.[7] Such an approach to personal "identities" in Imperial Germany is original in analyzing minority self-stereotyping as a discourse and instrument of ideology, and not as a form of self-hatred or mere "passing." Just because stereotypes of self-hating

Jews, hermaphrodites, homosexuals, and other *Others* were pre-eminent in late nineteenth-century Europe does not mean that they depicted real persons. Precisely because it was such an effective promotional tactic in the press and in book publishing, *Girl Years* and the history of its reception show that self-hatred is a label, indeed a *libel*, that can be affixed to any group or individual in any epoch.

II

To understand the conditions under which Baer's narrative was produced and interpreted requires drawing on genre-based and intertextual evidence that has inflected readers' responses – from low or "trivial" literature to advertising and book jackets. Such an approach involves both directly related textual references as well as less directly related cultural expressions, providing an impressive array of potential evidence.[8] This intertextual generic methodology permits us to answer both production- and reception-related questions: Why did Baer and those promoting him choose the particular subjects they did? What sources did these individuals draw on, what constituencies did they wish to engage, and what approaches did they exclude? And which pre-existing intertextual frames did readers use to make sense of the memoir, and were the meanings produced always in the interest of those social formations possessing more economic, political, or cultural capital?

One crucial intertext that Simon fails to acknowledge in his afterword is the social and literary sensation of Herculine Barbin, born in the French village of St.-Jean-d'Angely in 1838 and understood to be a girl until she reached the age of twenty-two – exactly the same age as Baer when she underwent surgery. At that time, according to his/her posthumously published memoir, Barbin fell ill and was examined by a doctor who, upon examining her somewhat ambiguous genitalia, determined that she was actually a male. Barbin was then forced to change his civil status. The phenomenon of gender variance (also known as "transgender"), though it might exist in nature, was still held under the law to be an impossibility. Ordained to live as a man, Herculine, now named Abel Barbin, killed himself eight years later.

It is rather likely that Baer, or at least his publishers, were familiar with Barbin's tragic narrative published in 1874. A century later, this "memoir" was reissued with an introduction by French philosopher Michel Foucault.[9] That edition, published in English in 1980, contains excerpts of the autopsy report as well as "A Scandal at the Convent," a fictional account of Barbin's life written by Oscar Panizza some years after Barbin's suicide. (On Panizza, see Chapter 2 in this book as well.) Foucault himself was drawn to the material inasmuch as it illuminates a time when society, reinforced by judicial systems and biological knowledge, began to define and enforce modes of sexuality. Opening his analysis with the now famous question, "Do we truly need a true sex?," Foucault projected his own hopes onto a past in which he imagined men and women were somehow less constrained in shaping their sexual identities and desires. At the same time, however, Foucault's case study represents an early challenge to the ideological dogma of "self-hatred." While flawed, his reconsideration of Barbin's memoir unsettles essentializing categories, an influence evident in *The Mystery of Alexina* (dir. René Feret), a feature film of 1986 which narrates Barbin's life.

The approach I propose here, then, examines self-hatred not only as a discourse governed by sociohistorical and intertextual contexts, but also as an effective tool for the promotion and circulation of books. There are several grounds for identifying self-hatred as discourse and marketing in the N. O. Body memoir. These grounds range from the biographical and compositional to the genre- and reception-oriented.

Baer's life, as best we can reconstruct it, substantially challenges the self-hatred hypothesis. In fact, the salient features of *Girl Years* are its multiple identities, multiple meanings, and multiple modes of address. The evidence suggests that Baer, as both Martha and Karl, was a reasonably well-adjusted person (or what present-day therapists would term "functional"). Although this distinction should not diminish the very real emotional pain experienced by Baer, his sensationalizing literary agent, Rudolf Presber (1868–1935), the author of humoristic fiction and editor of a popular magazine, denied the suggestion of self-hatred: "In amazement I listened to her life's story that was presented simply and free of pathos, without the bitterness of an accusation but with the restrained sorrow of an oppressive youth."[10] Baer's biographer, Simon, also eschews self-hatred as an explanation: "[Baer] was not psychologically stunted by his difficult childhood as a girl; he led a normal life as a capable and successful man who was a factor in public life and a prominent figure in the Jewish community" (i–ii). If indeed self-hatred were the issue, Baer might not have given us so many clues as to his real identity.[11] Discretion served merely to protect Baer's family, as his circumstances were already known by acquaintances and colleagues. Even catalogers at the Berlin University library knew the secret, penning in "Karl Baer" next to the author entry "N. O. Body." Indeed, Martha/Karl chose to remain permanently in Berlin, whereas he could have settled in Lemberg or elsewhere.

The careful construction of the N. O. Body memoir further rebuts the idea that Baer was psychologically scarred. *Girl Years* is not only a didactic narrative seeking to enlighten its addressees; it is also entertaining, aesthetically pleasing, and a quick read. At the same time, it is polysemic and multi-generic. For the author proves himself a master of popular literature, drawing on a hodgepodge of nineteenth-century genres: the autobiographical confessional, the narrative of uplift, the romance, the detective story, and the Freudian case history.

The influential possibilities of mass culture are thematized at the beginning of *Girl Years*.[12] N. O. Body also boasts that, as a grade-school "girl," he was writing essays for students who preceded him in social rank. He admires public speakers, debaters, and publicists as "demigods" (106), a factor in his preference for a journalistic career. As Martha Baer, he made numerous contributions to the bestselling German Jewish weekly ever: the *Israelitisches Familienblatt* (Israelite Family Journal), a non-partisan family journal read by at least fifteen percent of the potential Jewish audience in Imperial Germany. (For a more complete treatment of the *Familienblatt*, see Chapter 5.) In light of such evidence, it is difficult to have sympathy when Baer, after taking up a masculine identity, laments that he has no career possibilities. (Barbin makes a similar complaint in his book.) In fact, Baer's memoir was contracted before it was ever written, and it was destined to sell well under the tutelage of Presber, Hirschfeld, and others.[13]

In addition, Baer's struggle to become a writer is thematized throughout the memoir. His skillful command of popular narrative and understanding of social systems of distinction point to his later successes in public life and as an author. His journalistic production is still being uncovered, and no one has yet determined under what other pseudonyms he may have published other middlebrow works. (See, for instance, the obituary of Jewish activist Lina Morgenstern signed "N. O." in the Jewish cultural magazine *Ost und West*.)[14] In *Girl Years*, he develops a narrative economy marked by suspense, foreshadowing, and the interplay of desire and fear. The event-driven focus of his technique brings narrative flow to what might have become a staid memoir. Crucial in Baer's literary apprenticeship were the specific intertexts that informed his literacy. Excluded and shut out by her schoolmates, the nine-year-old Martha is said to have responded with a veritable reading fever, devouring magazines such as *Die Gartenlaube*, large quantities of loan library novels by Eugenie Marlitt and Friedrich Gerstäcker, and adventure stories about Indians, pirates, and the like.

Thirteen years later, in *Girl Years*, Karl Baer draws on a variety of popular fictional genres, the most obvious being the redemptional narrative of uplift. Baer's dedication of the memoir to his wife, Beile, supplements the trope of the benefactor who uplifts a talented young person. At the same time, the scenario is introduced with poetic sensationalism: "There were such deep wounds/As a knife could never cut/One can forget them, dream them away/ To heal them – this one cannot" (7). Yet the beloved soon comes to the rescue, disposing of the initial claim that "Norbert" (as opposed to "Nora") O. Body is unable to redeem his wounded childhood.

> This book is a book of truth. The strangest youth that was probably ever lived, speaks its own language here. This life is to be believed, as strange as it might be. To be strange, however, is not to tell lies. I want to speak in this book of a life that lay like a burden upon an unknown person until soft, white women's hands took the weight

from him and transformed his sadness into joy. It is the story of the
trials and conflicts that grew out of my most inner essence.
    I was born as a boy, raised as a girl....
    And the decision came as *the* woman came into my life. I also
want to talk about the love to this woman, who removed the thorns
from my path and who transformed my life....My entire life was like
a street filled with thorns – until I met her (8).[15]

The language and style of these first sentences recall the confessional genre,
and the promise of redemption issued here goes on to permeate *Girl Years*.
In keeping with his didactic project, the narrator draws a lesson after nearly
every episode as well as at the book's beginning and end. By alluding to the
thorn-crowned, suffering Jesus being comforted by Mary, the narrator
embarks on a rhetorical strategy aimed at drawing women into identifying
with the story. The narrator's continuous advice on raising children further
suggests that women readers were carefully targeted. Thus, the final insight
of the narrative insinuates that Baer's mother should have seen the emerging
"tough Jewish male" behind the cross-dressed façade. A "good" mother, it is
implied, would have enlightened her child and noticed the growing isolation
between ages nine and twelve, the lack of menstruation, and other external
markers. In retrospect, the narrator figures himself as a "tomboy," preferring
to play with boys, imitate cowboys and Indians, smoke, climb trees, and
build tree houses.
    While Baer's revisionist, essentializing argumentation reflects the domi-
nant discourses of Wilhelmine culture, the framing of these discourses in
specific genres is intended to appeal to readers.[16] Another genre evoked in
Girl Years is the rags-to-riches story of a poor shopgirl from a declining
wealthy family who becomes a women's activist and an academic. It is unlikely that Baer was actually apprenticed in a shop. Still, hoping to attract a
greater audience, the narrator makes a special effort at reconciliation with
the working classes: "Incidentally, young people from educated backgrounds
are often only more refined – not better – than those from the lower class"
(95).[17] Phrased as afterthought, this statement reinforces a mode of address
that conceals the author's class allegiances. At the same time, it suggests a
move toward class consensus designed to appeal to readers of varying
backgrounds in Imperial Germany.
    Two familiar genres even more central to *Girl Years* are the detective story
and the romance. The former appears combined with the Freudian case history. Baer devotes over a third of the memoir (nearly half if we include the
narrator's sexual fantasies) to the latter. The moralizing tone, more prominent toward the beginning and end of *Girl Years*, yields ultimately to the
love story. Nor does Nora O. Body lack for suitors (both male and female).
As in the "Tootsie" movie of 1983 starring Dustin Hoffman, the cross-dressing
male of *Girl Years* becomes a nearly voyeuristic observer of women's lives

and bodies. After falling in love with Hanna (*read*: Beile), Nora O. Body receives a series of absurd love letters from a male suitor. Later, she punches the young doctor who is treating her for depression when he makes a pass at her.

The modern strategy of diversifying genres to attract readers is reflected in the savvy promotion of *Girl Years*. As noted already, the book was a marketing coup, going through at least six editions within two years. At the price of 2.50 marks, it was affordable to many. Georg Rietz, Baer's publisher, pandered to a broad readership; his list of titles that same year included *Das Buch der jüdischen Witze* (The Book of Jewish Jokes). The book jacket to *Girl Years*, illustrated by Lucian Bernhard (an acknowledged leader in graphic design), was also calculated to appeal.[18] It is not surprising, then, that the cross-dressing narrator pays unusual homage to the professional window-dressers, who earn larger salaries than the store managers.

Baer's sixth sense for marketing suggests that the discourse of "respectability" (*Sittlichkeit*) in *Girl Years* need not be taken at face value.[19] In addition, the (post-Freudian) license to talk frankly about sexuality is balanced by a perceived need to cloak it in respectability. The openness of this Victorian-era discourse is consistent with Michel Foucault's account of nineteenth-century Western Europe in his *History of Sexuality*: the children know more than the parents, and sexual knowledge is circulated with astonishing speed. This scene of Wedekindian "spring awakening" is thus replete with N. O. Body's erotic fantasies.

III

The consensus of the publishers and agents of *Girl Years* – "[Baer] didn't write a thriller" – is disingenuous. For the individuals behind *Girl Years* set out to achieve the largest readership possible. It was a memoir discussed not only in literary and scientific journals but also in the popular press. What Simon calls the "lively resonance" of the text as well as its "lively portrayal" are at odds with his position that the integrity of the memoir is beyond question.

The 1907 foreword and afterword to *Girl Years* anticipate today's practice of excessive blurbs and book promotion. Consider as well the introductory note by Baer's agent, Presber, who becomes ever more sensationalistic in pitching the book, applauding its novelistic qualities: "I had the impression that nature, in league with a humanity enslaved by custom...had created one of those novels that varied between tragedy and comedy, a novel that no fantasy-filled narrator would dare to make up" (3). Magnus Hirschfeld, in his contribution, hopes that *Girl Years* "should find an audience far beyond medical and legal specialists" (163). The controversial Jewish sexologist declares the suicide of students and other youth tragedies to be real, not merely the stuff of *Trivialliteratur*. Yet, as his biographer Manfred Herzer has demonstrated, Hirschfeld was himself very much a public figure and an untiring self-promoter. Although Hirschfeld had already diagnosed Baer as a "pseudo-hermaphrodite," he enhances the appeal of *Girl Years* by referring to him as an "extreme hermaphrodite," an embodiment of the so-called "Third Sex" or sexual "intermediaries."[20]

The latest edition of *Girl Years* is a paperback on high-quality paper reprinted by Edition Hentrich. Although it is a dedicated anti-fascist publisher located in eastern Berlin, the Hentrich house chose to market *Girl Years* together with a series of detective and erotic novels by Rudolf Schlichter.[21] It is thus no accident that one of the first reviews of the newly reprinted memoir appeared in the conservative *Berliner Morgenpost*.[22] The reviewer for the *Morgenpost*, a daily newspaper directed at middle-class audiences, distorted the memoir and thus (further) sensationalized the story. It may also not be coincidental that *Girl Years* has been republished in post-Wall eastern Germany and that the German print and visual media have capitalized on the issue of "passing" in recent discussions of the GDR past.[23]

The approach to *Girl Years* in this chapter runs counter to current theories that proceed from linguistic or ideological suspicion. Rather than reducing Baer's memoir to the tenuous nature of the sign or a politics of power, I have interpreted it within its medial context. Readers should, for instance, beware of a Freudian take on this text, fraught as it is with phallic imagery, culminating in Baer's childhood fantasy of being the snake Chingachgook from James Fenimore Cooper's *Last of the Mohicans*.[24] (It is true that Baer explicitly identifies with Oedipus and Achilles, but only inasmuch as the former was sent off to the mountains and the latter grew up in girl's clothing.) Historians will also recall that Freudian analysis (e.g. *The Interpretation of Dreams*, 1900) was itself an established genre by the time *Girl Years* was released in 1907.

As a result, Baer's veiled references to his misshapen penis at times make the leap from "kitsch" to "camp," as does the occasional irony in the text. It is so playful that, if anything, I have in this essay underemphasized what might be termed "the pleasure principle" of *Girl Years*. Baer as a narrator indulges in public spectacle, a type of performance that would have become intimately familiar to a person engaged in role-reversal over the course of three decades. My reading is only one of many possible readings that would emphasize the pleasure of multiple identities in *Girl Years* and its considerable investment in the activities of identity formation. Baer's representations of desire and masochism in reading, writing, and learning additionally recall a number of postmodern and postcolonialist modes.[25]

As evidenced in *Girl Years*, autobiography and memoir are themselves unstable narrative modes. Over twenty years ago, Hayden White pointed out in his *Metahistory* how the necessarily language-bound form of historiography operates to fictionalize its own referents. In the meantime, historians have been undertaking a rigorous interrogation of the stories they write, producing accounts and theories that question the possibility of objective historical representation.[26] I would only caution that the rules of evidence still apply when attempting to analyze events and lives. Consequently, my conclusions here – however "emplotted" they may appear – are constrained by the historical evidence.

Despite the spectacular, sensationalist qualities of *Girl Years*, qualities as evident to Baer's contemporaries as they are today, I have endeavored to interpret Baer's memoir with restrained sympathy. This seems to me to stand in contrast both to Foucault's and to Judith Butler's interpretations of Barbin's memoir. There are doubtless many individuals for whom such fragmentation is torment, and Butler may be correct that Foucault's study of the hermaphrodite tends to gloss over pain and romanticize Herculine's multiple pleasures.[27] At the same time, one need not accept Butler's account in its entirety. Perhaps in part influenced by the 1986 film or the memoir's fateful dénouement, she is compelled to write that "we fail to discover multiplicity, as Foucault would have us do; instead, we confront a fatal ambivalence, produced by the prohibitive law, which for all its effects of happy dispersal nevertheless culminates in Herculine's suicide."[28] For Butler – and in her reading, for Foucault – power and sex are coextensive. That is, because the law generates sex, there is no possibility that Herculine could be "subjected" to heterogeneous pleasure in some safe realm beyond power.[29]

What seems to me to be lacking here is a more finely grained, differentiated account of narrative. Even if Butler's analysis of Barbin and of Foucault's distortions is accepted, the historical subject "Karl Baer" was not the same as the historical subject "Herculine Barbin." Butler herself, just a year after her critique of Foucault on Barbin, delivered a long apologia recognizing how self-hatred can be as much trope as truth. In an extensive, unusually personal comment, she confirms that "[t]o call another person self-hating is itself an act of power that calls for some kind of scrutiny."[30]

Girl Years then should be read not only by conventional intellectual historians, but also by cultural historians and practitioners of mass culture studies. Multivalent, multigeneric narratives such as Baer's challenge notions of intrinsic textual meaning. In a book on James Bond films, influenced by the Birmingham school of cultural studies, Tony Bennett and Janet Woollacott conclude that reading is not a process "in which the reader and the text meet as abstractions but one in which the inter-textually organised reader meets the inter-textually organised text. The exchange is never a pure one between two unmediated entities."[31] To do justice to the N. O. Body memoir and its readers therefore means to see them as the product of a complicated dialectic between intertextual and social determinants. This dialectic crosses German, Jewish, and gender boundaries. Yet it ultimately rejects a suspicionist discourse of tragic self-hatred. A similar approach, we shall see in the next chapter, is productive when interpreting Kafka's writing and *its* multiple border crossings.

4

FRANZ'S FOLK(LORE)

Kafka's *Jewish* father complex

Return to the father. Big Day of Atonement. (*Rückkehr zum Vater.
Großer Versöhnungstag.*)
                                     Kafka's diaries (September 28, 1917)[1]

I found just as little rescue from you in Judaism. Here rescue would
have been conceivable. But even more, it would have been conceivable that we both could have found ourselves in Judaism or that
we could have started out united from there.
                                     Kafka's famous letter to his father, 1919[2]

[P]sychoanalysis emphasizes the father-complex, and some find the
concept intellectually nourishing...[Yet] I prefer another version,
where the issue revolves not around the innocent father, but around
the father's Judaism.
                                     Kafka (letter to Max Brod, 1921)[3]

I

In this chapter, I will explore directly Kafka's own private "kitsch." By that,
I am referring to Kafka's own personally inflected adaptations of popular,
especially Eastern, Jewish culture. These include the adaptation of popularized Kabbalah, especially early Hasidism, as mediated to Kafka by individuals (Jiří Langer, Yitzchak Löwy) and through reading (e.g., of Martin
Buber as *the* middlebrow mediator of Hasidic tales). Finally, this middlebrow popularized Kabbalah – Kabbalah itself already marked as heretical
and anti-hegemonic – made it possible for Kafka to rework discursively not
only his own Judaism (both as culture *and* religion) but also his (less well-
known) gender ambivalence.

In this mode, Kafka's textual and personal denials of Jewish knowledge
operate according to a logic of dissimulation.[4] No doubt, such dissimulation was also capable (paradoxically, perhaps) of resulting in Jewish

"dissimilation," i.e., *anti-assimilationism*. The objective of such dissimilation was to achieve a certain authentic Jewishness. At the same time, this dissimilation acknowledged its own inherent rhetoricity, thus enabling Kafka to reinvent Judaic traditions by means of a discursive self-awareness. From his first longer work, "Das Urteil" (The Judgment, 1912) to his final one, "Josefine, die Sängerin oder das Volk der Mäuse" (Josefine, the Singer: Or, the Mouse-Folk, 1924), Kafka's narratives are characterized by a sense of irony and nuance, even comedy. And it is by such means that Kafka came to terms with "his role as a writer in and for the 'Volk' of assimilated Jewish Germans."[5]

My approach of uncovering concealment and dissimulation brings together two relatively recent approaches within Kafka Studies: namely, Kafka as "Judaically literate" (*pace* Max Brod, Gershom Scholem, Robert Alter, Karl Erich Grözinger, and Walter Strauss) and Kafka as "homoerotic," if not "homosexual" in practice (Mark Anderson and Evelyn Torton Beck).[6] I thus contend that Kafka concealed his non-normative sexuality through the trope of Judaism. According to Reiner Stach, one of the recent biographers of Kafka: "Even if the initial impulse behind his [Kafka's] asceticism was fear of sex, the fear does not account for the single-mindedness with which he clung to asceticism for the rest of his life or in the highly imaginative manner in which he subjugated one area of his life after another – eventually even literature – to an ascetic form."[7]

Yet from where did this "single-mindedness," a recurring problem in research on Kafka, emerge? What are its sources? In the following considerations, I wish to illuminate some of the (surprisingly) *popular* Jewish sources of Kafka's "aesthetic asceticism."

II

The veiling of the father's body...takes a variety of forms in [ancient] Israelite religion: the prohibition on making images, the aversion of the gaze of characters who see God, and the submerging of the listener's perspectives into the perspective of God. This cloaking of the deity's sex, the invitation to be a virtuous son of Noah, calls for a new way of thinking about what has traditionally been regarded as a growing Israelite discomfort with anthropomorphism.[8]

This is how Howard Eilberg-Schwartz, a historical anthropologist, locates ancient Judaic culture in a double-bind between love of a male God and homophobia toward His body. Such a tension was relieved by veiling and/or not representing the divine body. At the same time, Israelite men were to be portrayed as "feminine" – for example, through having been circumcised – in distinction to surrounding cultures.

Eilberg-Schwartz thus only confirms what was in rabbinic Judaism (the "Talmud") at least a *minority* tradition and, in Kabbalah and Hasidism, a *majority* tradition. Following Sigmund Freud (1856–1939), he contends that the fear of male-to-male erotic relations results in a distancing of the (most) beloved Male into the authoritative Father figure: "When a man confronts a male God, he is put into the female position so as to be intimate with God. The masculinity of Israelite men was thus most secure when God turned his back, hid his face, or kept himself covered in a cloud or in the heavens."[9] And glossing Freud's *Totem and Taboo*, written at the same time as Kafka's literary breakthrough, Eilberg-Schwartz and others focus on Freud's suppression of the consequences of Oedipal desire. For if a male child does not desire to kill the father in order to possess the mother, he might also become the "passive" recipient of the father's sexual desire. Being thus placed in the stereotypical "feminine position" similarly makes intimacy with the deity possible in both normative (or rabbinic) Judaism and Jewish mysticism (or Kabbalah). While human masculinity was strongly associated with procreation in ancient Israelite culture, men were in time understood to have been created "in the image of" a divine parent. This was a parent, however, who was considered to be celibate or even *beyond* sexuality.

The Hebrew Bible, which Kafka came to know well, uses marriage and sexuality as metaphors for describing the divine–human relationship.[10] Kabbalah, read as a series of texts about envisioning God, uses a similar system of erotic symbolism, according to Elliot Wolfson.[11] One of the leading living interpreters of Jewish mysticism, Wolfson describes how men in Kabbalist circles constructed their gender identities in ambivalent terms. Historian David Biale has chronicled the ambivalence experienced by the successors of these men, the earliest Hasidic rabbis (to whom I will return at the conclusion of this essay).

But this longstanding Judaic ambivalence *was* mediated to Kafka, who in turn articulated it in his own reworkings of texts as diverse as biblical and Midrashic parables, Hasidic tales, and popular Yiddish dramas. (As noted in Chapter 1, Kafka was so enamored of the Yiddish theater after being first exposed to it in 1911 that he rarely attended other types of theater thereafter.) Kafka's early protagonists, especially in what he termed his three stories of "sons and fathers" – "The Judgment," "The Metamorphosis," and "The Man Who Disappeared" – vacillate between expressions of loving devotion to god-like father figures and (hetero)sexual concerns deemed egotistical.[12] Just as Moses may not contemplate God naked, so too do Georg Bendemann, Gregor Samsa, and Karl Roßmann recoil from the literal or figurative sex of their overdimensional father figures. The Holiness Code of Leviticus similarly links three distinct prohibitions: against making material images of God, against undressing one's parents, and against violating heterosexual norms. For Eilberg-Schwartz, the figure of Moses articulates a very general rabbinic anxiety about the conflict of being married to an earthly woman and loving a deity who is male. Kafka's own anxiety corresponds closely, alternating between living (*Leben*) and writing (*Schreiben*), the latter characterized by him at one point as "a form of prayer."[13] This form of devotion is reflected as well in his much-cited claim in the letters to Felice that he was "nothing but literature."[14]

While the male fear of homoeroticism is inscribed in Judaic (and other) traditions, Judaism also has resources for interrogating homophobia and heterosexism. It is important to remember that the modern (Zionist) idea of the tough, masculine Jew was an anachronism prior to the nineteenth century. Up until that point, at least among East European Jewry, the gentle, "effeminate" Talmud scholar (or *yeshiva bokher*) functioned as the cultural ideal for men. This figure commonly served as a marriage – and potential erotic – object for Jewish women.

In the limits of this chapter, I can only outline how Kafka was influenced "consciously and unconsciously" by the historical problematic of an embodied male God. This deep structure influenced Jews over the *longue durée* and, as outstanding scholarship has demonstrated in recent years, it is a fundamental problem that is reflected in the work and lives of other *fin-de-siècle* European Jews such as Freud. It also provides a perspective from which to approach and to unsettle two related binaries in Kafka scholarship: "eroticism versus asceticism" and "clothing versus art."

According to Mark Anderson, being in the realm of "clothing" is equivalent in Kafka's writings to being bereft of or exiled from the sacred.[15] Put differently, the realm of uncovering brings one, in Kafka's art, closer to the realm of the holy. It is suggested by the verse epigraph to his earliest extant text, *Description of a Struggle*: "And people go strolling in clothes/ swaying on the gravelly path/under the great heavens...."[16] Anderson goes on, in an essay based on a reading of Kafka's unabridged diaries (available only since 1990), to offer an explanation of the relationship of religion to asceticism in the writer's life and art. To be sure, Kafka's notorious *disgust* with sexual relations fits conveniently into Max Brod's image of his friend as a "a saint who eschew[ed] all earthly temptation for the sake of his writing."[17] That said,

> disgust is precisely what is lacking in Kafka's characterization of desire between men. Though it may provoke a variety of emotional responses ranging from simple affirmation and childlike fascination to near-sublime moments of terror and pain, homosexual desire does not trigger the same order of emotional denial that the mere thought of marriage and heterosexual relations induced.[18]

Anderson describes how Kafka's *oeuvre* is informed by "[t]his same discrepancy between 'disgusting,' 'animallike' heterosexual intercourse on the one hand, and seductive, eroticized fantasies about powerful men on the other."[19] To this account, I would add that the fantasies of powerful men are also informed by longstanding Judaic discourses. Kafka's homoerotic fantasies and the dilemma of an embodied male God, I contend, also fit more than "conveniently" (Anderson's term) into his image as a religious writer and/or asexual ascetic.

The relationship is complex between embodied authors and their sexual fantasies, on the one hand, and disembodied aesthetics and a transcendent deity, on the other. An incorporeal deity is clearly a problem when we attempt to conceptualize gender and sexuality, the source of conflicted images of masculinity in the history of monotheism. Because the divine–human relationship was often described in sexual terms – when "Israel" follows other gods, "she" is seen to be whoring – homoeroticism became an issue in ancient Israel. At the same time, the metaphorical feminization of these "Children of Israel" (or *b'nai yisrael*) is at the core of Judaic patriarchy: it is human males, not females, who are imagined to have the primary intimate relations with God.[20] For the disembodiment of a father-like God was also problematic in a culture in which human men are not expected to be sexless, but rather to reproduce despite having been created "in the image" of a God who is figured as celibate.[21] The emphasis on earthly male procreation continued to coexist uncomfortably in later Judaism with the valorizing of asceticism, most notably in medieval mystical literature. Halakhic Judaism today still expresses the problematic of an embodied deity insofar as observant men are required whenever praying to wear a garment covering up the penis. In addition, the transmission of *halakhic* law (i.e., Talmudic learning) is equated with the fathering of children. Indeed, a man's teacher is regarded as more important than his parents.

In the canonized version of the Hebrew Scriptures, the ambivalence about God's sex is indicated most forcefully when Moses intentionally averts his gaze as God – upon Moses' requests – reveals himself in a physical manifestation. In passing before Moses (in Exodus 33), the deity permits the prophet to see His body, but only from the rear. This matter is crucial for Eilberg-Schwartz: "The word that is rendered as 'my face' (*pānāy*) is more equivocal than translations suggest. *Pānāy* can also mean 'my front side.'"[22] In turn, a later prophet becomes party to what is the most extensive "God-sighting" in the Bible: Ezekiel is permitted to gaze upon the deity's loins. In another episode (Genesis 6), which has brought commentators to despair, angel-like "sons of God" (*b'nei Elohim*) have sexual relations with earthly women. And that episode can be productively compared to Lot's encounter with those angelic guests whom the men of Sodom wish to get to know (to *know* in the "biblical sense" as well). As, in Sodom, earthly males are seeking intimacy with divine males, Lot's offer of his daughters is read by Eilberg-Schwartz as yet another "attempt to turn the desire of human men away from men of God [and] back to appropriate objects: human women."[23]

III

I have described Eilberg-Schwartz's argument in such detail in order to clarify the reading of Kafka's early works which follows. In interpreting these autobiographically inflected fictions, it is important to attend to the aspects of uncovering and homoeroticism in Genesis, specifically the biblical narrative of Noah. While one might argue that Noah's son Ham observed his father's nakedness by an accident, gazing usually "generate[s] desire" in the Hebrew Bible (as well as in Talmud and Midrash) inasmuch as the male gaze and desire were "linked in the ancient Israelite imagination."[24] Isn't Georg Bendemann's gazing at his father, who in Kafka's "The Judgment" is explicitly standing "erect" in bed, to be linked with *desire*? And with *passivity*, as rabbinic interpreters saw Noah as adopting what was considered to be a "female" position?[25]

After all, "The Judgment" (1912), the acknowledged turning point in Kafka's career, is the first time in his *oeuvre* when a father figure becomes larger-than-life. The elder Bendemann, having been initially portrayed as "toothless," is described as "huge" when he suddenly stands upright on his bed. This symbolism is so patently Freudian that Kafka himself wrote of the story: "Thoughts of Freud, of course."[26] After asking insistently whether he is "covered up" well, Georg's father becomes the focal point of the story in what is clearly its most decisive turning-point:

> "No!" shouted the father...flung back the blanket with such forces that for an instant it hovered unfolded in the air, and stood upright in the bed. Against the ceiling he held one hand lightly. "You wanted to cover me up, I know, my little fruit, but I'm not yet covered up. And even if I'm at the end of my strength, it's enough for you, more than enough."[27]

A relationship between uncovering and homoeroticism is suggested by the manner in which the father's tirade continues: "Of course, I know your friend. *He* would have been a son after my own heart. That's why you've been deceiving him all these years."[28]

For seasoned interpreters of Kafka, Georg's friend in Russia has remained a figure of mystery. But he is undeniably part of a three-way relationship with the son and the father, the homo*eroticism* of which is difficult to ignore. According to his father, Georg also "should never have gotten engaged" to a woman when he already has such a wonderful friend, a friend whom the father defends vigorously, indeed with a certain excess. The friend's positive connection to the divine is then suggested by Kafka's diary record of Hasidic–Kabbalistic lore, in which (male) angels (compare the comments on Lot and Sodom above) are said to accompany those who are pious whenever possible. In the case Kafka cites, angels are said to have escorted to heaven a

Hasidic miracle-working rebbe who had lived, precisely like Georg's friend, in a "far-off Russian town."[29]

The striking image of Georg's father standing with his hand against the ceiling already associates *him* with a higher, deific power.[30] One thinks of Kafka's fanciful diary entry in 1914 of an angel who suddenly bursts into a room through the ceiling. Those and other associations with the divine in "The Judgment" recall the father's ultimate sentencing of Georg to death by drowning, a judgment most notably found in the Hebrew Bible when God executes the same verdict upon the generation of Noah.

Such judgments are almost inevitably associated in Judaic tradition with Yom Kippur, the annual Day of Atonement (see the first epigraph to this chapter.) It is well-known that Kafka wrote "The Judgment" in the night of September 22–23, 1912, in the immediate aftermath of Yom Kippur that year (on September 20–21). What is less well-known is that Kafka's *father's* birthday was September 14, a day conventionally close to annual observances of Yom Kippur. What is almost completely unknown – at least to many non-Jews – is that the afternoon (or *minchah*) scriptural reading for Yom Kippur (Leviticus 18) is taken directly from the so-called Holiness Code about forbidden sexual relations. But it is an odd choice of scripture, as Jews have noticed for centuries; Kafka probably noticed as well. The portion (or *parashah*) is all the more curious as it is one of the few prohibited under rabbinic law for public study. (It might only be read out loud at a Torah service.) In fact, the portion may have originally been chosen because it reflected a tradition outlined in the Talmud (specifically in *Mishnah Ta'anit* 4: 8), according to which Yom Kippur (along with the Fifteenth of Av) were among the most joyous days in the Judaic calendar. At the appointed time, young women would dance in the fields before young men who would then choose brides from among them. According to a related tradition, the solemn mood of Yom Kippur ended with the early afternoon (i.e., *minchah*) Temple ritual, whereupon the "assumed forgiveness and absolution of the people was celebrated through dance and courtship."[31] It was to remind the people not to get carried away during the dancing that this Torah reading was chosen.

Georg Bendemann likewise gets "carried away" in "The Judgment." As his father's capacity for divine-like judgments is progressively revealed, so too does Georg become progressively feminized: he virtually "mothers" his sick old father at the story's midpoint and, by the end, he has been rendered passive – to the point of accepting his father's fatal verdict. In addition, Georg is symbolically penetrated: he not only bites his tongue during his father's harangue, but his ear reverberates especially (on his way to the site of his suicide) with the echo of his father's uncovered body falling back onto the bed.[32] In Kafka's private and public writings, the frequency of such images, often accompanied by knives, indicates a wish to be penetrated.[33] The most famous image of penetration may be the conclusion to *The Trial* in which the main character, Josef K., is stabbed to death, "like a dog" (in his own suggestive words).

Yet such figurative feminization is not a negative value for Jewish males. The rabbis of the Talmud understood that, in the relationship with God, men were to assume the position of wives. Later sages at times read Scripture "as if they imagined themselves as women, looking to female models for how they should behave."[34] These effeminate models included the biblical figure of Joseph – the name of the protagonist in *The Trial* – in certain respects comparable to Karl Roßmann, the protagonist of Kafka's suggestively titled *The Man Who Disappeared* (published in part as *Der Heizer* in 1913).

Not only was the thought of seeing God a decidedly erotic experience, but in time all observant Jews came to be perceived as feminized *vis-à-vis* the deity. The commandments to be obeyed were thus represented as "women's ornaments." Arguably, the most important such "ornamentation" in Judaic tradition was thought to be circumcision (*b'rit milah*).[35] In rabbinic Judaism, circumcision was regarded as a

> prerequisite for God's appearance to men....Through the act of circumcision, one may stand in the presence of God....not only because circumcision is a sign of the covenant, but also because men may meet God only as women.[36]

Masculinity, then, was *God's* to define. Encoded for the ancient Israelites as "a symbol of male submission," circumcision acknowledged God as "the ultimate male" in whose presence human masculinity was seen to be compromised.[37] Kafka's diary entries on circumcision in 1911 are particularly extensive.[38] And circumcision is (at least) a subtext of "In the Penal Colony" (composed in 1914). The main figure of the novella, the Officer, celebrates a male order that uses a unique apparatus executing punishments – and inscribing the precise verdict! – upon the bodies of those deemed guilty of a transgression. At the same time, the Officer maligns what he sees as the overly *feminized* order of the New Commandant, an order which puts the Old Commandant's "life's work" at risk.[39] The significance of gender and sexuality to the novella is apparent. Moreover, "In the Penal Colony" like "The Judgment" originated at the time of Yom Kippur (October 1914).

Daniel Boyarin argues that circumcision is not always a metonymy for castration in Freud's thought.[40] Instead, Boyarin demonstrates the opposite: *castration* was nearly always a symbol of *circumcision* for the Jewishly self-conscious Freud. But one need not proceed from this premise in order to recognize that Freud was Kafka's contemporary, another (sensitive) Central European Jew whose thinking – both "conscious" and "unconscious" – was informed by similar forces and discourses. Indeed, if we concur with Eilberg-Schwartz's premise, Kafka's homoeroticism actually manifested that which Freud ultimately repressed in himself. *Moses and Monotheism*, a partial culmination of Freud's thought, draws "a connection between the father-hood of God, the prohibition on images, sexual renunciation, and the triumph of the spirit over the senses." Specifically, Freud figures "the prohibition on images" to be connected with male asceticism.[41]

Freud thus preferred to read the prohibition on images of God as a "triumph of spirituality over the senses."[42] If he had not, however, fully disavowed his homoeroticism, Freud too might have interpreted the Judaic prohibition on images as a means of veiling the body of the Father God.[43] For the human father's sexual body is otherwise central in Freud's account of the Oedipus complex. And even though it is absent in *Totem and Taboo* and *Moses and Monotheism*, the relationship between the image of God and homoerotic longings for fathers was explored by Freud in other contexts, most notably in his case studies. The most salient example is that of Daniel Paul Schreber, a (non-Jewish) appellate court judge in Leipzig. Freud's analysis of Schreber's case in 1911 is where sexuality and religion are most clearly linked.

In his personal memoirs of hospitalization in two asylums (written between 1900 and 1902), Schreber develops a detailed theology in which he imagines that God wishes him to be transformed into a woman. He refers to this transformation as "soul sensuality" (*Seelenwollust*), an attempt to transcend sexual desire by becoming both woman and spirit. Schreber observed changes in his own body: a retracting male organ and feminized breasts and hips. Disturbed initially by this transformative "unmanning" (*Entmannung*), Schreber gradually came to terms with his desire to cultivate feminine feelings.

Schreber and Freud were likely familiar with the resonances of the term *Wollust* from the Lutheran translation of the Bible into German. The biblical matriarch Sarah, when informed that she will conceive a child at ninety, asks (sarcastically) whether she should at her age truly "cultivate sensuality" (*Wollust pflegen*). Kafka too may have understood the resonances of *Wollust*. In a diary entry on "The Judgment" of February 11, 1913, he uses the term to describe Georg's (homoerotic relationship) to the friend in Russia: "The friend is the connection between father and son, he is that which they have most in common. Sitting alone by his window, Georg revels with desire (*Wollust*) in this commonality."[44] Later, in composing "The Metamorphosis," Kafka portrays to Felice the writing process as "an extremely sensual business" (*äußerst wollüstiges Geschäft*).[45] Some critics, in fact, have noted the closeness between Gregor Samsa and his nearly eponymous sister, Grete, maintaining that Gregor desires to become a woman. Schreber too wished to develop a womb in order to conceive, and Kafka claimed that "The Judgment" emerged from him "like a regular birth, covered with filth and slime."[46] Similarly, when metamorphosed into a vermin, Gregor succeeds in "enwombing" himself. This enables him to look like the woman in furs whose image is introduced on the very first page of the novella. As a wish-fulfillment of the desire to be female, this same magazine photo is later enveloped by Gregor with his insect body.

Whereas Schreber felt rays or energies penetrating and entering him, Gregor is bombarded by his father – himself *transformed* into a stronger, godlike figure – with apples. One of them penetrates and embeds itself in Gregor's back. A few sentences later, Gregor loses his eyesight (symbolic for the castration complex) at the precise moment his mother loses her petticoats, one after the other, so as to merge "in complete union" (*in gänzlicher Vereinigung*) with the father.[47] When Kafka conceives of being "united" (*einig*) with his own father, he writes (in the infamous "Letter to [the] Father"): "I found just as little rescue from you in Judaism. Here rescue would have been conceivable. But even more, it would have been conceivable that we both could have found ourselves in Judaism or that we could have started out united from there."[48] Such Oedipal scenes of union as the fictional one (cited immediately above) from "The Metamorphosis" therefore encompassed more than homoeroticism for Kafka.

In 1921, Kafka addressed psychoanalysis directly, writing to Brod that "psychoanalysis emphasizes the father-complex....[Yet] I prefer another version, where the issue revolves not around the innocent father, but around the father's Judaism."[49] Prior to coming to terms with his own homoeroticism, Freud had considered and then abandoned his "seduction theory," choosing to imagine the "father's innocence" by conceiving of both his own and the *divine* father as lacking sexual/reproductive organs. Freud's own working through of the father complex corresponds with the period (1911–13) in which he was also dealing with (his own) homoeroticism and (his own) Judaism. Eilberg-Schwartz thus maintains:

> It is significant to note that just prior to Freud's second fainting spell in Jung's presence, he and Jung were discussing monotheism. The conversation revolved around a paper by Karl Abraham...on the ancient Egyptian Amenhotep IV (Ikhnaton). In his essay, Abraham anticipated many of the concerns Freud would later take up in *Moses and Monotheism*, for he [Abraham] gives an analytic account of monotheism's origin. When Freud fainted, Jung was disagreeing with him about whether there was a father complex behind the creation of this monotheistic religion, a point Abraham had made in his paper.[50]

In particular, Freud fainted as Jung suggested that Ikhnaton did not harbor hostility toward his father but in truth revered him to the highest degree.

IV

Karl-Erich Grözinger has clearly detailed how Kafka reiterated different strands of popularized Kabbalah. I am arguing in this chapter that Kafka reiterates different, but no less significant, strands of Jewish culture existing *prior* to Jewish mysticism. In comparison to the Freud of the fainting episode, Kafka appears to have been more open to minority traditions in the history of Judaic civilization. It is in this sense as well that his work time after time unsettles the conventional opposition of asceticism and eroticism.[51] Indeed, Kafka wrote in his diary on September 25, 1917 (close to Yom Kippur and his father's birthday): "Return to the father. Big day of atonement." The telling pun here – that the German word for atonement (*Versöhnung*) also contains the word for son (*Sohn*) – refers both to the Day of Reconciliation (Yom Kippur) and to the process of becoming a *son*.

In addition, Grözinger describes an entire literary genre in which the kabbalist seeks to eliminate his carnal desires by means of extreme asceticism. Kafka too took cold baths and performed a regimen of calisthenics naked in front of an open window. Revealingly, he found something akin to his ideal of body culture during his Jungborn nudist holiday in the summer of 1912, the setting for some of his most homoerotic experiences. Kafka wrote to Brod from there that he was also in the process of "lamenting to myself...which is how devout women pray."[52] Finally, Kafka's ideal of "ascetic marriage," outlined in his diaries, requires "coitus as a punishment for the happiness of being together. To live as ascetically as possible, more ascetically than a bachelor – that is the only possible way for me to endure marriage."[53]

At the same time, both Kafka's work and the Kabbalah valorize a type of displaced eroticism. By the advent of Hasidism, numerous sources report how the *shekhinah* – the divine presence, a feminine (almost Marian) representation of the godhead – replaces the wives of the pious when they are worshipping or studying; she literally "unites" with them.[54] To the devoted unmarried "kabbalist," explains Grözinger, human women are regarded as temptresses distracting him from saintly thoughts and pursuing him "into his dreams, thereby causing involuntary and sullying ejaculations."[55] This sublimated asceticism has its early counterpart in the *Zohar*, where an authentic *unio mystica* is achieved through a unique "kiss of death." This is directly noted by Kafka in his diary in his synopsis of Pinès' reading of I. L. Peretz's story "Kabbalists": "*Mitat neshika*, death by a kiss; reserved only for the most pious."[56]

Peretz's story is from a collection entitled *Khsidish* that deals intensively with Hasidism, and it is no secret that Kafka was an avid reader of Hasidic tales. In a letter to Brod, Kafka noted that the stories were "the only Jewish thing in which I invariably and immediately feel at home, irrespective of my mood."[57] Like others of his generation, he became familiar with the tales of the Baal Shem Tov (the "Besht") and Reb Nachman as mediated via Buber and others.[58]

In the stories told about him, the Baal Shem Tov (the founder of Hasidism) prefers abstinence to (hetero)sexuality. The same can be said of his descendents, such as the Maggid of Mezerich, Dov Ber, who practiced a combination of mystical union and sexual renunciation.[59] The most important Hasidic figure for Kafka and others was almost certainly Nachman of Bratslav, whose early life was as focused toward asceticism as to ecstasy, according to Buber.[60] A more recent commentator writes:

> Of all the Hasidic masters, Reb Nahman appears to have most inherited and perhaps even intensified the standard kabbalistic approach to gender. Indeed, Nahman was one the greatest Hasidic interpreters of the Kabbalah; in particular the theosophical material of the Zohar and Lurianic writings. From Nahman's statements, one sometimes get the impression that he would have liked to avoid contact with women entirely Yet the very act that apparently most terrified Nahman – intercourse with a woman – was required of all Jewish men in order to be fruitful and multiply.[61]

V

In closing, we should note Kafka's description in his diaries of his friend Jiří Langer's rabbi, the Hasidic Rebbe of Belz. After visiting the Belzer court with Langer (who was incidentally gay himself), Kafka noted how the rebbe's underwear could be seen under his caftan. The description is *not* to be taken literally, but is informed by an eroticized discourse of uncovering God the Father: "Underpants visible..... Hair on the bridge of the nose. A fur hat which he continually moves back and forth. Dirty and pure."[62] For Kafka, the rebbe became simultaneously pure and sullied, both ascetic and erotic.

If we agree with little else in Freud, we can accept that he was correct in contending that images of authority figures, both divine and parental, are inevitably entangled. As Eilberg-Schwartz concludes, "the possibility of connecting to divine images, whether male or female, clearly is related to the relationships we have to our mothers and fathers."[63] The same may hold true for Kafka, especially as a turn-of-the-century sensitive Jewish male of the same generation as Freud. The reading I have presented gives an important gloss to the "assault against the last earthly border" (*Ansturm gegen die letzte irdische Grenze*), to which Kafka refers in a January 1922 diary entry after a nervous breakdown. In particular, my interpretation may provide additional insight into the writer's immediately subsequent diary entry, a much-quoted remark about a new Jewish discourse:

> This entire literature is an assault against the borders, and it would have – if only Zionism had not gotten in the way – easily been able to develop into a new secret teaching, into a Kabbalah. There is already movement in this direction.[64]

Kafka makes clear in his diary that the assault in question may not only emerge from below, from "humanity," but that it may also come down, from "above."[65]

At this moment in 1922, Kafka also began writing *The Castle*, a fragmentary novel characterized by the search for admission to a court which seems to be located beyond "earthly boundaries." In addition to the apparent bisexuality of K., the land surveyor, in his scenes with Bürgel, any interpretation of the novel must account for the sexual prowess of the godlike figure of Klamm. Like the castle itself, Klamm cannot be sighted, only heard or read (the latter by way of written communiqués). In a very specific sense, this later narrative by Kafka appears to be working through a *Judentum* (which is as religious as it is cultural or ethnic).[66]

In Kafka's metaphor of a boundary-crossing assault, his impatience with the present state of Judaism is readily apparent. The near apocalyptic tone of his writing at this point is meant to indicate a phase of transition. As he put it, in an unpublished text: "I have taken up strongly the negative of my era. It is indeed very close to me; I do not have the right ever to fight it; to some extent I represent it. In its least positive aspect, as well as its most extreme negative (switching over again to positive), I had no inherited share....I am end or beginning."[67]

Whatever the nature of the boundary crossings from "The Judgment" to *The Castle*, Kafka was careful to project his heteronomic discourse of Jewishness, a re-mediated and popularized Kabbalah, onto his ambiguous gender identity and concealed homoeroticism. These heteronomic, at times apocalyptic, moments are also responses to political and social developments affecting Jews in Central Europe, developments to be discussed in the following chapter.

5

POGROM IN... *BERLIN*?

Working through the Weimar Jewish experience in popular fiction

Why are there no pogroms in Germany? Because the Germans would first *form a line* in order to buy tickets (joke told by East European Jews in the era before World War I).[1]

I

The examples of popular culture to be addressed in this chapter are the installment (or serial) novels that appeared between 1922 and 1923 in the most widely circulated Jewish newspaper of Weimar Germany, the *Israelitisches Familienblatt* (Israelite Family Journal). Like other such mass media, the *Familienblatt*, published weekly in Hamburg, Frankfurt, and Berlin between 1898 and 1938, has rarely been analyzed by historians of German-speaking Jewry. This neglect is conspicuous because the *Israelitisches Familienblatt* was *the* bestselling Jewish periodical in early twentieth-century Germany.

The *Familienblatt* is also an especially representative source. First, it considered itself a "family journal" (*Familienblatt*), part of a tradition inaugurated by Ernst Keil's *Die Gartenlaube* (founded 1853), the most popular German-language periodical of the nineteenth century.[2] Second, it endeavored to be non-partisan, distancing itself from political Jewish organizations, such as the Zionists and, to a lesser extent, from the more assimilationist *Centralverein deutscher Staatsbürger jüdischen Glaubens* (Central Association of German Citizens of the Jewish Faith). Third, it was completely financed through advertising and subscriptions. It was thus imperative that it sell itself, and sell itself it did. It found a significant resonance in the German-Jewish community, reaching *at least* fifteen percent of the potential Jewish market in Germany (ca. 600,000) – a high figure for any mass publication.

While purporting to understand German-Jewish lives and mentalities between 1918 and 1933, scholars have omitted not only the periodicals most popular with Weimar Jewry, but also the installment novels and other fictions that appeared between their pages. Unlike memoirs, letters, and other more researched sources, representative German-Jewish journal literature provided its targeted constituencies with the illusion of "community," that is, with a rhetorically constructed "ethnic" Jewish identity. In this fictional but very public sphere of the serial, an overarching consensus was sought. This consensus embraced the broad nature of Weimar Jewish social formations ranging from established upper middle-class to Jewish proletarians and migrants from Eastern Europe.

At the same time, the installment novel was a serious response to the social realities of Weimar-era Jews. No mere pulp fiction (or *Trivialliteratur*), stories in the *Israelitisches Familienblatt* engaged dialogically with the world around them. That writers as disparate as Meta Opet-Fuß and Martin Salomonski felt compelled to address similar phenomena – class distinction, refugees, prostitution, and broken families – confirms as much. These serial novels thus demonstrate that the public debates of German Jewry often reflected their interior lives and experiences. For German-Jewish popular culture was not imposed from without or above, but constructed from within and below. As serialized fictions mediate the range of attitudes and fantasies that are acceptable to a collective group in a specific epoch, they add significantly to our knowledge of the social and cultural history of that group. These and other texts found in popular magazines and newspapers reflect the myriad ways in which German Jews understood themselves as both "Jews" and "Germans."

Installment novels such as those of Opet-Fuß and Salomonski are perhaps more "Jewish" than one is led to expect by the scholarship on Weimar Jewry in which narratives of assimilation predominate. Writing in response to this teleology of decline, Marion Kaplan maintains: "What has become a paradox for historians appeared reasonable and consistent to the German Jews themselves: they were at one and the same time agents of acculturation and tradition and of integration and apartness."[3] Michael Brenner has also recently shown that Weimar Jews, even if they did not identify with Zionist or Orthodox communities, were not nearly as *un*-Jewish or *anti*-Jewish as intimated in the work of earlier scholars. To be sure, fictions targeting Jewish middle-class readers and fictions directed at the non-Jewish middle class had much in common. But whereas German middle-class values were prevalent in the Jewish propertied and educated bourgeoisie (*Bildungs- und Besitzbürgertum*), its members – from daily tea and evening leisure to weddings and holidays – mainly interacted with other Jews. This much was true for those Jews who were highly acculturated or had converted to Christianity.[4]

What the *feuilleton* fiction confirms is that Jews in the Weimar Republic developed independent ways of coping with problems of everyday life. Their survival strategies were also embodied in symbolic cultural practices, especially narrative. In addition, what matters is not how closely the serialized stories were read, but rather that they were constructed in such a way that Jews would identify with them. For some of the best clues we have for Jewish mentalities in this era are embedded in the stories that Jews told *each other*, stories performed for a German-Jewish audience in a German-Jewish space.

II

"Versöhnung" ("Reconciliation"), the first of the two novels to be discussed, was written by Meta Opet-Fuß, a Breslau-based Jewish writer. It dominated the *Feuilleton* section of the *Israelitisches Familienblatt* between October 12, 1922 and July 12, 1923. Little is known about Opet-Fuß or her works. As we shall see, her Jewish communal politics probably did not differ substantially from those of the *Israelitisches Familienblatt*. More significant, however, is the relationship of "Versöhnung" to the assassination of German foreign minister Walther Rathenau by antisemitic nationalists on June 24, 1922. The murder of Rathenau, a Jewish German and the first foreign minister of the troubled Weimar Republic, explains in part why the editors of the *Israelitisches Familienblatt* decided to run an installment novel after publishing short stories in previous months. Nor was this to be any ordinary installment novel for the journal. In a preview dated October 5, 1922, the editors assure us that "Versöhnung" (displayed in huge type) "will meet with appreciation and attention" among regular readers as the novel "gives expression, in extremely vivid and inspiring fashion, to the idea of reconciliation (*Versöhnung*) between Jews and Christians" (p. 9).[5]

Indeed, the three months between the assassination of Rathenau and the appearance of "Versöhnung" suggest that the serial was specially commissioned for the *Israelitisches Familienblatt*. Clearly the product of a particular cultural–historical configuration, the action of the novel takes place in a Berlin reeling from revolution and civil war in the early 1920s. The young protagonist, Adolf Thalheim, is a Jew, a writer, and a weakling (an apparent twentieth-century descendant of Bernhard Ehrenthal of Gustav Freytag's *Soll und Haben*). Adolf's best friend, Fritz Dietrich, is a blond-haired, blue-eyed student and gymnast (*Turner*). The young Jew's father pressures him to give up academic pursuits and (finally) become a businessman; Fritz's father, a well-known professor, preaches antisemitism at the dinner table. While Adolf proves unfit for the *Wandervogel*, a German youth association, his "Aryan" friend leads a *Wandervogel* troupe of students on hikes and nature outings.

Fritz is a philosemite, however, and thus embroiled in conflict with his father. In addition, he is secretly enamored of Adolf's sister, Eva. She personifies the "beautiful Jewess" (*la belle juive*) of lore. In part to be near her, he teams up with Adolf to establish an organization, the League of Reconciliation (*Bund der Versöhnung*), which institutes gymnastic lessons for (physically challenged) Jewish males.[6] The integrity of the League is put to the test when Adolf confronts four closet antisemites in the group. When challenged to a duel, Adolf rises to the occasion. His courageous death in the ensuing shootout leads one of his enemies to renounce antisemitism. When the Christian Fritz is denied the ultimate reconciliation, i.e., inter-marriage with Eva, he nonetheless carries on the struggle for civil rights in order to fulfill his friend's ideals and redress his father's wrongs.

In addition to possessing all the elements of a popular genre fiction, Opet-Fuß's "Versöhnung" was interested in creating *consensus* among its almost exclusively Jewish readership. Consensus was projected all the more urgently when there seemed to be few grounds for it, here in the first major crisis years of the Weimar Republic. The title alone speaks volumes. Forging con-sensus through *reconciliation* forms the central moment of "Versöhnung." Yet what types of consensus take place here and in other serial novels pub-lished in the *Israelitisches Familienblatt*? While Jewish/non-Jewish reconci-liation is often thematized, a reconciliation *between* Jews was more popular. In particular, the extremes of the Jewish middle classes, which became even *more* extreme in the late Wilhelmine period, are seen as in need of consensus.

Such consensus is commonly brought about in these fictions through marriage. Indeed, the largest source of *Israelitisches Familienblatt* revenues were the advertisements for marriage partners. And a careful examination of these *Heiratsannoncen* (marriage advertisements) suggests that social har-mony, i.e., a good dowry and a good match, was the primary motivator for such advertisers and respondents. Trude Maurer, in an analysis of these "personals," estimates that the predominant group of readers were owners of retail stores, followed by white-collar employees and sales representatives. (In this framework, one might think of Kafka's protagonists, particularly the traveling salesman Gregor Samsa.) A smaller subgroup consisted of owners of large businesses. Rarer were manufacturers and factory owners, at least until the 1920s, as well as teachers, Jewish communal workers (*Kultusbeamte*), and academic professionals.[7]

More microcosmic consensus takes place within fictional Jewish families, leveling not only the gender gap, but also the *generation* gap separating parents from their children. Deviations from the family norm in fictions from the *Israelitisches Familienblatt* are the old maid aunt and the bachelor uncle. Reconciliation of Jewish husbands and wives is supposed to overcome the threat of marital collapse. In particular, the turning-points of the novels center around Yom Kippur, the Jewish day of atonement (in German, the "day of reconciliation" or *Versöhnungstag*). The type of reconciliation sig-nified here is decidedly Jewish, and it likely would have been understood as such by *Familienblatt* readers while allowing for differences in their levels of Jewish cultural literacy and religious observance.

Just how precarious reconciliation actually was between Jews and non-Jews, Jews and other Jews, and Jewish men and Jewish women is under-scored by the fault lines that emerge in "Versöhnung." In this respect, the

66

characters are more plausible than public Jewish figures such as Rathenau. Also at stake in Opet-Fuß's novel is the female romance writer's typical desire for revenge, as outlined in Tania Modleski's *Loving with a Vengeance.*[8] According to Modleski, "domestic novels" reveal a covert longing for power. Beneath highly orthodox plots, these and other mass-produced narratives for women contain elements of resistance to consensus and reconciliation. Modleski contends that "women writers of popular fiction have registered protest against the authority of fathers and husbands even while they appeared to give their wholehearted consent to it."[9] Opet-Fuß's foregrounding of the strong sister at the expense of the weak brother in "Versöhnung" can be read as an objection to that authority and the less domestic, more acculturated lives of middle-class German-Jewish males. It is no coincidence that the author ("Meta") offers readers so many opportunities to identify with her artistic counterpart and near-namesake "Eva."

But male readers are, contrary to expectation, included in such identifications. This is underlined when the Thalheim parents have a revealing fight over their children. At the climactic close of installment 13, Mr. Thalheim asks his wife: "Do you think it's possible that Eva will get over this critical stage as easily as you did?" (December 29, 1922 installment 9). The answer comes at the start of the next episode:

> "I don't think so," rejoined Mrs. Thalheim. "As you know, she has a lot more energy than I do. If she has the same amount of talent – which of course remains to be seen – then she won't desist from the goals that she sets for herself." "Even if I had been more strict, it probably wouldn't have helped. You're probably right," added Mr. Thalheim. "If my parents had been more understanding of my poor brother, then maybe he'd still be living in our midst," said Mrs. Thalheim. What her daughter had said had made her think.
>
> January 4, 1923, installment 10

Whereas the narrative perspective of the episode may privilege Eva, male readers too are invited to identify with her through the repeated associations with her uncle, a talented actor and role model. As a result, both sexes could be persuaded of the novel's plausibility inasmuch as the dialogue of women characters is (almost without exception) more convincing than that of men.

Although fissures appear in "Versöhnung," at times undercutting social reconciliations, they also serve to make the plot more plausible. The forty installments of the novel are a visible response to historical developments, and at least one major shift in the plot can be traced. Throughout the first three-quarters of the novel, there is little unevenness. The flow of the narrative suggests that Adolf will become a successful writer, that Fritz will marry Eva, and that the extended family Thalheim will be reunited and live in harmony ever after. By all indications, a happy ending is on the way.

But at this point the typeface changes abruptly and the print size is reduced. Although it may only be a printer's error, it is not inconceivable that Opet-Fuß was compelled to rewrite and add new exposition. In any case, the tragic deaths and near non-consensus of the last quarter of the novel belie the positive expectations generated. This circumstance, however, makes "Versöhnung" more believable than comparable serial fictions from the *Israelitisches Familienblatt*, including Salomonski's novel (discussed below). The final chapters may also be characterized as a response to a perceived rise in antisemitism.

Consider the second-to-last installment of June 28, 1923, where Adolf's sister Eva rejects Fritz's proposal to wed. Even though he has just declared his willingness to convert to Judaism in order to marry her, she replies

> It's not right to give up so much for me....You'll find a more deserving woman. You see, we Jews want to get along with everyone, but we don't want to give up our Jewishness and be absorbed into the world around us. Oh, I know there are lots of Jewish girls out there who would marry a Christian, even if he wasn't willing to become a Jew as you are. But I'm one of those who couldn't get over the contradiction involved in denying the existence of the Jewish people intellectually – somehow seeing being Jewish as just a religion – while at the same time feeling part of a national community [*Volksgemeinschaft*] deep in my heart. Jewish women are especially attached to the traditions handed down to us, traditions that in the seclusion of the ghetto, over the course of centuries, became flesh and blood. When you're brought up Jewish, there's simply something you have in common with other Jews that can't be put into words. It makes all Jews related to each other in some way, and makes most Jewish girls want to marry a fellow Jew. This of course doesn't prevent Jews and Christians from marrying, as is now so often the case, as long as – "As long as the heart is in the right place," added Fritz. Eva was silent for a long, long time. Then she said, visibly moved, "I really didn't know that you were in love with me. Another man came first and won my heart. He is a Jew; he is actually the brother of my mother...."
>
> June 28, 1923, installment 9

The subtlety of Eva's own romantic ambivalence is quite remarkable for a serial fiction. And what began as anti-defamation is rendered believable by recourse to a permissible variant of Jewish marriage. For Eva's nearly incestuous engagement to her Uncle Karl is not as implausible as it may seem at first glance. One must recall that Judaic restrictions on marriage within the family applied primarily to members of the immediate nuclear family. However, almost all types of cousin marriages between Jews were permissible according to *halakha*, and there was even a preference in some circumstances for patrilateral parallel cousin marriage, i.e., a union between the children of two brothers. There was no explicit rule against marriages between uncles and nieces in spite of aunt/nephew prohibitions (Adolf's relationship to his aunt is depicted as friendly but aloof). In fact, the Talmud and other rabbinic commentary were predisposed to such marriages on the assumption that they would be more affectionate.[10] Such unions – at least in the realm of fiction – were not a far-fetched response to the perception of increasingly anti-Jewish activity in 1923 Germany.[11]

That even stronger responses would be required is evident from the final paragraph of "Versöhnung," two installments later. Here, social reality appears to give way to social hygiene as Fritz addresses his father and the Thalheims:

> We Germans are strong in body and soul, and if you really want to be German Jews, then there shouldn't be any of you who think that training the body is unimportant. You're also going to have to integrate yourselves among our laborers, our artisans, and our farmers to the same extent you've done so among our learned men and business people. I have made this undertaking my life's goal, Herr Thalheim, and from now on I will work to bring about a reconciliation between Christians and Jews. The End.
>
> July 12, 1923 installment 4

For readers today, such rhetoric sounds racialistic. And, as noted already, readers led to expect full-scale reconciliation might have been taken aback by calls for the restructuring of Jewish occupations. Nonetheless, there are cultural and political grounds for the belated emphasis on the apologetics of physical fitness in "Versöhnung." These grounds in turn confirm a striking correspondence between serial fiction and the social imagination. The notion that Jews should become farmers and artisans and/or improve their bodies had been around since the (German) Enlightenment.[12] It is fair to say that German-Jewish youth, by the Weimar period, had internalized such stereotypes to some extent, including the idealization of being active in the outdoors. The bulletins of the Liberal youth movement were "full of letters in which idealistic Jewish youngsters explained to their worried bourgeois parents or to 'effeminate' brothers why they went for one-week hikes, slept in tents, and ate from tin plates."[13] By the 1920s, about one-third of all young German Jews, Zionist or non-Zionist, belonged to one of the Jewish youth organizations.

After "Versöhnung" appeared, Opet-Fuß continued to be involved in anti-defamation, authoring essays on Jewish sport and on Jews and pacifism that appeared in acculturationist Liberal Jewish publications.[14] In fact, defending the faith (and the "race") became the most important agenda for Jewish-directed media and fiction after 1918. Although most prevalent in the statements of the Centralverein, this ideology of anti-defamation was quite nuanced and varied. To Zionists and their opponents alike, much immediate post-World War I activity was spent dispelling legends, such as the myth that Jews had shirked military service or the myth of a Jewish, leftist "stab in the back"(the so-called *Dolchstoßlegende*).[15]

The discourse of anti-defamation took on a particular urgency amid the historic events of 1922 and 1923, indicating a wish for fantasies of reconciliation. Since 1918, Germans had experienced civil war, an inflation-fueled recovery, and further dislocations. In addition, Rathenau's assassination was one of several murders of leaders of Jewish descent, including Rosa Luxemburg, Kurt Eisner, and Gustav Landauer.[16] Thomas Mann's youngest son, Golo, could thus remember the "joyful noise we schoolboys made when we learned about [Rathenau's] assassination."[17] Later, in his historical writing, he concluded that antisemitism was stronger between 1919 and 1923, in the years of hyperinflation, than it was in 1933, the year Hitler came to power.[18]

After "Versöhnung" had been appearing for three months, French troops occupied the Rheinland and Ruhr. The German response to this was "a great upsurge in nationalist outrage," which was legitimized and exacerbated by the Weimar government's declaration of a policy of "passive resistance."[19] To ensure that the production goals prescribed in the Treaty of Versailles would not be achieved, the government of the Reich financed a general strike in the Ruhr region, subsidizing the salaries and wages of workers and public employees. Separatist violence and acts of terrorism were concurrently on the rise.

By the summer of 1923, it was clear that passive resistance in the Ruhr would fail, yet reactions to it were (at least obliquely) reflected in the week-to-week composition of "Versöhnung." The January 11, 1923 installment of the novel suggests such a condition: When Adolf proposes the idea of his League of Reconciliation to his Jewish employers, they prove lacking in vision, responding with ridicule. Their rejection, exacerbating Adolf's depressed state, moves the novel in a different direction. This episode seeks to demonstrate that an overly commercial orientation among Germany's Jews was detrimental. Adolf's Jewish employers, depicted as indifferent to their young charge's aesthetics and politics, represent the old guard of the Centralverein. In contrast, Adolf proposes a new variant of Centralverein ideology, aligned with the need for anti-antisemitic agitation and propaganda.

Subsequent events further affected the composition of the next installments of "Versöhnung" and contributed to the complex, negotiated ending of the novel cited above. In the summer following the Ruhr crisis of 1923, nearly all Germans, from wage-earners to those on fixed incomes, were fighting a losing battle with hyperinflation. In addition to an alarming increase in cases of tuberculosis and rickets, a rise in anti-government disturbances culminated in emergency degrees in Bavaria in September 1923.

Just two months after "Versöhnung" ended in the *Israelitisches Familienblatt*, attacks on "Jewish-looking" passers-by took place in Beuthen, an ethnically mixed industrial area in Silesia. Although these "excesses" began as food riots in the wake of shortages and higher prices, they came to involve several hundred people.

The town of Beuthen was fifty kilometers from a place called Oświęcim, better known today by its German name, Auschwitz.[20] That said, it remains problematic to engage in "backshadowing" in order to uncover some kind of cause-and-effect relationship between the early 1920s and the Holocaust. For around the same time, an editorial signed by a number of prominent figures appeared in a leading newspaper: "The undersigned, citizens of Gentile birth and Christian faith, view with profound regret and disapproval the appearance in this country of what is apparently an organized campaign of anti-semitism...The loyalty and patriotism of our fellow citizens of the Jewish faith is equal to that of any part of our people."[21] The newspaper in question, however, was *The New York Times*; the country, the United States.

IV

By October 1923, East European Jews were being expelled from Bavaria and, starting on November 5, the notorious Scheunenviertel riots (*Scheunenviertelkrawalle*) took place in Berlin. The Nazi newspaper, *Der völkische Beobachter*, made the exaggerated (and *fore*shadowing) claim that the unrest in the Scheunenviertel pointed toward a "coming storm."[22] The facts were that, over the course of two days, thousands of young men rioted, looted, and assaulted passers-by in the streets of the Scheunenviertel.[23] Regardless of whether one calls it a *pogrom*, "[i]t showed how easily and quickly socioeconomic frustrations could boil over into anti-Jewish violence."[24] It also indicated how broad antisemitic sentiment was in post-World War I German society, at least among right-wingers.

The perception of rising anti-Jewish sentiment and violence is reflected in the very next serial fiction which appeared in the *Israelitisches Familienblatt*, Rabbi Martin Salomonski's "Die geborene Tugendreich. Ein Großstadtroman" (The Woman née Rich-in-Virtue: A Metropolitan Novel). Tacit in Salomonski's novel, for all its oblique references to antisemitic acts, is the recognition that it had become virtually impossible by late 1923 to publish a novel about Jews set in the present. The option remaining was a historical novel, in this case set in 1903 during the boom years of Imperial Germany. Until the stabilization of the Weimar Republic in 1924, it appeared that a reconciliation between Jews and non-Jews was no longer realizable in the framework of a contemporary fiction.

Whereas "Versöhnung" falls short in achieving consensus, "Die geborene Tugendreich" fails at times to be plausible. Realistic motivation and psychological causality are not always manifest even though the novel was

71

published as a separate book five years later. More importantly, "Die geborene Tugendreich" seems to have been specifically formulated as a counterpoint to "Versöhnung" and its agenda of reconciliation. A desire for lighter, more escapist fare in times of crisis had been prefigured in the announcement for the novel, issued a week before the first installment:

> In the next issue we begin with the publication of our new novel, "The Woman née Tugendreich" [printed in large type] by *Martin Salomonski*. It is set in Berlin in the prewar era, when the flow of life was so much more unhurried and tranquil than it is today. With its empathy and friendly humor, the novel depicts a circle of lower middle-class [*kleinbürgerlich*] Jewish families, revealing how young people with their newfangled plans and ideas bring trouble and turmoil to contented precincts. The main characters have something of the gentle and dreamy quality that so distinguished Georg Hermann's unforgettable [novel] *Jettchen Gebert*.
>
> August 2, 1923, p. 4

This mode of address targeted actual (or would-be) lower middle-class readers, socially positioned between the working-class and upper-middle-class characters featured in the novel. The work also touched a nostalgic nerve in accord with a general longing among Weimar Jews for the "good old days" of the Wilhelmine era. For, more than ever before, the white-collar core audience of the *Israelitisches Familienblatt* found its socioeconomic status on the decline. In line with the practices of the time, these subscribers (themselves occasional advertisers) also favored arranged marriages over romantic coupling. "Die geborene Tugendreich" compensates *them* by delivering a rags-to-riches love story.

Minni, the daughter of the Jewish-born-but-intermarried Regina Witt, is presumed to be a non-Jew of working-class background and thus inappropriate for marriage to Dr. Max Rosenthal. By extension, she is inappropriate for his class- and caste-conscious parents, Jettchen and Jonas. In a series of elaborate episodes, the Rosenthals' milieu of theaters and cafes (central Berlin, i.e., Mitte/Tiergarten) is juxtaposed with the Witt's simpler pleasures and less deluxe haunts (Berlin-Friedrichshain). True reconciliation is made possible only when Minni turns out to be Max's first cousin. For she is the eponymous "geborene Tugendreich" of the novel.

As a congregational rabbi, the author of "Die geborene Tugendreich" was eminently qualified to understand Weimar Jewry's conflicts and consensus. Salomonski was born in Berlin in 1881, where he also earned a doctorate at the Liberal rabbinical seminary (the *Hochschule für die Wissenschaft des Judentums*, where Franz Kafka would later audit courses). After holding a pulpit in Frankfurt on the Oder and serving as a military chaplain in World War I, he returned to work in his home town in 1925. As a literary man of the cloth, Salomonski went on to publish other prose fiction, including a 1934 fantasy about life in Palestine, *Zwei im andern Land* (Two in Another Country).

"Die geborene Tugendreich" is in many respects informed by Salomonski's biography and career. Indeed, Max's self-characterization as "the linguist who deserted 'rabbinism'" (October 11, 1923, installment 4) could apply equally to the Liberal Jewish *Doktorrabbiner* Salomonski. Thus at times, the protagonist seems to be a wish-fulfillment, capable of almost anything. Having turned down the rabbinate and achieved academic prominence, Max also modernizes the family business by upgrading office equipment and instituting other innovations.

The twists and turns of "Die geborene Tugendreich" are similarly resolved in a modern (yet Jewish) manner. Although love conquers all in the end, Max and Minni are technically first cousins. Yet what might have been deemed illicit under German law is superseded by the aforementioned Judaic partiality toward matches of uncles' children. And once again, Yom Kippur (the Jewish Day of Atonement) serves as an archetypal moment at which all tensions – familial, marital, and intergenerational – are overcome. Jettchen ends her opposition to the young couple's matrimony upon meeting Regina at religious services. Jonas is inspired by the High Holy Day sermon of Rabbi Krausnicker – who just happens to be a friend of the Witts – to reconcile with his brother for the disgrace he had caused the family by getting Regina pregnant years earlier.

Here and elsewhere in Salomonski's novel, consensus and reconciliation seems hard to achieve. And while it cannot be substantiated that "Die geborene Tugendreich" was modified according to the sociopolitical climate of Germany in 1923, the idea that Salomonski was composing installments of "Die geborene Tugendreich" just days ahead of their publication is not so speculative. In his history of American serial authors in the same epoch, James L. West documents the widespread practice of contracting for serial rights on the basis of an incomplete manuscript, often less than *one-quarter* complete. If an editor sensed potential in the completed chapters and the synopsis of those remaining, the magazine or newspaper would purchase the serialization. After receiving an advance, the author would compose subsequent chapters, collecting further paychecks as later chapters were delivered against specific deadlines. Frequently, the early installments were published before the final chapters had even been drafted.[25]

This well-established routine may explain why promises of the promotional teaser for "Die geborene Tugendreich" (quoted above) went unfulfilled. Salomonski's serial fiction, no matter how buffered it was from events of the day, reflects the "disorder and early suffering" (to borrow the title of Thomas Mann's novella) characterizing the early crisis years of the Weimar Republic. The novel's first sober, pessimistic installment (October 4, 1923) comes near its midpoint, just a week after the first reports had reached the

Jewish press of the riot-like situation in Beuthen. A mood of confusion is hinted at in the final images: melancholic and drunk, Max drifts through Berlin in the small hours of the morning, lamenting the misery of the world.

In the same episode, the limits and possibilities of German-Jewish symbiosis are rendered more equivocally than before in "Die geborene Tugendreich." After drinking and singing a German folksong ("Blonde Maid, komme zu mir") in the city's *Ratskeller*, Max and his Jewish comrades retire to a café in the Scheunenviertel. This establishment, dubbed "Lecho daudi" (Hebrew for "come, my beloved," taken from the Sabbath liturgy), is owned by a Germanified Eastern Jew (from Romania) whose "steel-blue eyes" enable him to preserve order in his chaotic saloon.

More important than this extraordinary portrait of an *Ostjude* is that it is the first time that East European Jews are referred to in an *Israelitisches Familienblatt* serial novel since (at least) prior to "Versöhnung." Although Regina originally hails from Poland, perhaps from Posen like so many other Jewish immigrants to Berlin, she is never explicitly described as an Eastern Jew. Minni, for her part, believes herself to be a Gentile, although the reader learns she is actually of German-Jewish paternity. Yet in the installment of October 25, 1923, Minni is assisted at the spa by a young woman with the Yiddish-sounding name of "Etla Fisch." While this can be taken as a reference to *Ostjuden*, Fisch is put in her place as an Eastern Jew, being said to lack "proper boarding-school training" (4).

That this was a time of political disarray for Jews (and non-Jews) in the *Reich* is further alluded to in the unusual episode of November 8, 1923, in which Jettchen goes to confront Max's girlfriend in Friedrichshain. Met by Minni's formidable (step)grandmother, Jettchen engages in a type of verbal violence. Grandmother Witt defends Minni's virtue against Jettchen's attacks, but Minni grows distraught and collapses, injuring herself, even losing blood. The "violence" expands in the next-to-last chapter (November 22, 1923). Here, a jealous, non-Jewish suitor, relatively new to the novel, attempts to shoot Max and Minni. The Scheunenviertel pogrom of previous weeks is almost certainly being cited, a notion validated by texts surrounding "Das geborene Tugendreich" in the *Familienblatt*. In a fantasy dénouement, the attacker is beaten down with a stick by Minni's half-brother (also a non-Jew). The final installment is a tempered happy ending, not unlike the breaking of glass that concludes a Jewish wedding and recalls the destruction of the Temple. "For happiness does not always laugh at the darlings of fate and there came the time which, as old Ezekiel said, engraved itself with crying and sobbing and lamentation" (November 29, 1923, installment 5). At the same time, the first major crisis of the Weimar Republic was being defused (if not forgotten) as the deportations of Eastern Jews inaugurated in Bavaria were soon renewed only days after the unsuccessful Hitler Beer-Hall Putsch of November 9.

In contrast to Adolf Thalheim in "Versöhnung," however, Max Rosenthal is represented as strong and in control of his surroundings in "Das geborene Tugendreich." Indeed, there is only one significant obstacle to his development, namely his mother. While the anti-feminism of "Die geborene Tugendreich" is somewhat assuaged by its context in a historical novel, Jettchen epitomizes the *yidishe mame*, a caricature with an infamous history in Jewish and *German*-Jewish letters. (It is arguable whether this example was truly inspired by Hermann's *Jettchen Gebert* which also appeared originally in serialization.) For Jettchen in Salomonski's fiction has the dubious honor of functioning as the primary source of conflict and misunderstanding. Max, despite recognizing that he has internalized some of her traits, is repeatedly victimized by her intrusions. Neither is his father spared. This results in a sentimentalized episode of "male bonding" between Jonas and Max, described using *mame loshn*, i.e., Yiddish.[26]

The portrayal of women and East European Jewry in "Die geborene Tugendreich" underscores the more convincing social dynamic of "Versöhnung." Jettchen's foil and the model female in Salomonski's novel is Regina, the Polish-Jewish mother of Max's fiancée. While praising Minni and her mother as women of valor incapable of "betray[ing] the tribe" (September 6, 1923, installment 9; and September 14, 1923, installment 5), Salomonski's narrator is also issuing a disguised attack on the virtue of East European Jewish women. It is, moreover, an attack that rehearses the discourse of the fallen Eastern Jewish woman victimized by the "white slave trade." This and other passages appear to blame East European Jewish women for their involvement in prostitution, notwithstanding the efforts of Bertha Pappenheim, Martha Baer (discussed in Chapter 3), and others to liberate them from it. As an example, the narrator directly addresses women readers at the novel's midpoint, issuing a proscriptive agenda for Jewish womanhood:

> Minni's evenings were not that exciting. But whoever means well by her won't lament that she usually stayed at home and hardly went out alone. Even a very confining home is the be-all, end-all for a woman if she's able to appreciate the greatness in small things. Comfort can be replaced by domesticity....See to it in your wisdom, you mothers, that your daughters and all young women have something they can hold onto in the quiet of their own worlds. A woman can only feel alive when she is able to dispense love in tiny ways.
>
> October 11, 1923, installment 4

Salomonski's apparent favoring of confining domesticity for women, a discourse typical of mass culture fantasy novels, stands in stark contrast to "Versöhnung." Understanding Opet-Fuß's novel as the woman writer's protest against such confinement is yet another way to take serial fiction seriously as a response to the social realities of Weimar Jewry. "Die geborene Tugendreich" not only imagines a different positioning of male readers but also elicits a variant of the putative "male gaze." For Max, it is important that he project "courage and decisiveness" when speaking to Minni for the first time in public. After a successful encounter, he feels like a "victor" for the rest of the day (October 11, 1923, installment 4). In contrast to Opet-Fuß's novel, Salomonski's opus betrays a more androcentric "style." At times, its incredible plot line permits action to supersede description and dialogue, resulting in a near stereotype of genre fiction.

IV

Compared to "Versöhnung," Salomonski's *Familienblatt* novel is less reliable but no less helpful as a guide to the experiences and self-understanding of diaspora Jews in a troubled phase of their history. Despite significant work already done on the Jewish experience in the Weimar Republic, we still need comparisons with other novels by the same authors, as well as with other installment fiction published in the forty-year history of the *Israelitisches Familienblatt*. *Feuilleton* novels for Jews were published in a number of venues, and it is possible that the theme of reconciliation appealed more to readers of the *Israelitisches Familienblatt* than to readers of other Jewish periodicals. The *Familienblatt*'s readers were also more likely to be Jews in small towns than city slickers, more likely to be families with small businesses than the *crème de la crème*, more likely to be non-observant than Orthodox, and more likely to be of middlebrow tastes. Last but not least, the readers were more likely both women and men: the placement of serial novels following the women's pages (*Frauenbeilage*) of the *Familienblatt* suggests as much.

The installment fictions discussed here also need to be understood in the larger German context in which non-Jews were publishing serialized novels.[27] More systematic research is also needed on the genres and techniques of installment fiction and popular literature generally.[28] The label *Trivialliteratur*, besides its negative association with women, has (unfortunately) proven to be as durable as any other stereotype. Critics of the ideology of mass culture (such as Theodor W. Adorno and Max Horkheimer) contend that this type of literature was informed by "reactionary" nineteenth-century models of middle-class Realism.[29] What may surprise the opponents of popular culture is the fact the narrator of "Versöhnung" more than once makes a transition between the middlebrow and the "meta" level (of self-reflective narration). Particularly overt are the parallels between the author (Opet-Fuß), the narrator, and the protagonist Adolf, whose efforts to become a writer are the subject of frequent excurses.

With its occasional self-referentiality, the *feuilleton* literature analyzed in this chapter constitutes an object lesson for today about the complexities of reading and reception.[30] By focusing not just on events themselves but on how they are represented and remembered, an integrated approach to the German-Jewish experience also reminds us about the complex relationship between narrative and history. Yet because in the wake of the Shoah the two are so difficult to distinguish, I will return to them in the next (and final) chapter on the writing of Germanophone Jews *after* the Holocaust.

6

AFTER THE "SCHOAH"

Performing German-Jewish symbiosis today

In pinpointing a key dilemma in the field of German-Jewish studies, Karen Remmler has recently remarked that "[d]espite all the talk about difference, about metaphor, and about text, scholars in the field...are still facing the dilemma of how to describe the way that a changing German-Jewish symbiosis might operate in the flesh."[1] By this final chapter of the book, it should be evident that German-Jewish "symbiosis" is more than Gershom Scholem's one-sided and all-too-lachrymose tale, an impossibility somehow mythologized "after Auschwitz."[2] To "flesh out" how post-Shoah German-Jewish relations operate requires a model that accounts for both embodiment and representation, assuming (with Remmler) that we have "agreed to agree about the very presence or possibility of a symbiosis in the first place."[3]

In lieu of a conventional concluding chapter, I will examine here a set of "embodied" (indeed, *eroticized*) representations from recent fictions by German-Jewish writer Maxim Biller. One of the best-known contemporary writers in Germany, Biller was born in 1960 in Prague and has resided since 1970 in the Federal Republic (formerly West Germany). In particular, I will juxtapose Biller's short fiction, "Finkelstein's Fingers" (1994), with the recent theorizing of philosopher Judith Butler on subjectivity and performativity. A comparison of these two contemporary writers and (former) *enfants terribles* – one of German-Jewish *belles-lettres* and criticism, the other of American Jewish feminist and queer theory – enables a productive discussion of comparative identity formation.

According to Jonathan Freedman, it is

> remarkable how many of the most profound revisionary thinkers of the performative – Derrida, [Shoshana] Felman, [Eve Kosofsky] Sedgwick, [Stanley] Cavell, Butler – are themselves Jewish-born scholars who have made glittering careers in canonical fields (philosophy, literary criticism, "theory") by carving out a space for alternative predications of identity, whether philosophical or sexual.[4]

78

Biller, I will argue, is very implicated in similar projects of articulating alternative identities as his writing attempts to tease out processes of identification
from their imbrications in processes of *constraint*. Biller's characters perform
a deviation from "German" (and "non-Jewish") norms, for constraining
interpellations of identity – in Butler's terminology, "reiterative convocations"[5] –
can never be completely enacted. As we shall see, the realization of such
confining interpellations is limited by Biller's "love–hate relationship" with (non-
Jewish) Germans as well as with the elements of "Germanness" in himself.

I

To synthesize conflicting moments of discourse is an objective of Butler's
theory of performativity. The considerations that follow concur in part with
her synthesizing insight that "all identities operate through exclusion,
through the discursive reconstruction of a constitutive outside and the production of abjected and marginalized subjects."[6] Yet, at the same time, such
identifications do not operate uniformly. This holds not only for gender
identities but also for ethnic and racial ones, as noted by Butler since the
publication of *Gender Trouble* (in 1990).[7] Once identity has been reconceived
as an *effect*, something produced or generated, possibilities for agency are
opened up that had been "insidiously foreclosed by positions that take
identity categories as foundation and fixed."[8]

Hence, Jewish self-stereotyping (or self-satirizing) in Biller and elsewhere
is better approached not as a sociopsychological pathology of "self-hatred"
or "assimilation" but as a discursive instrument of performativity. (Butler
herself has delivered a long apologia that recognizes how self-hatred can be
as much trope as truth. In an extensive, uncharacteristically personal note,
Butler writes that "[t]o call another person self-hating is itself an act of
power that calls for some kind of scrutiny."[9]) Similarly, one can read the self-
defensive irreverence of Biller's "Seeing Auschwitz and Dying" ("Auschwitz
sehen und sterben") in his earliest collection, *When I'm Rich and Dead*
(*Wenn ich einmal reich und tot bin*) as performing a mocking defiance. This
particular disposition, often captured by the term *chutzpah*, is most notably
celebrated by the American-Jewish novelist Philip Roth. As a major influence on many (Jewish) writers, Roth's popular postmodernist insistence on
multiple narratives is also echoed in contemporary German-Jewish writing.
In a variation on the adage "two Jews, three opinions," it is declared in
Operation Shylock (1993) that "inside every Jew there is a *mob* of Jews,"
each one of whom possesses a "manifold personality" that consciously and
unconsciously clamors for self-expression.[10] With its self-referential intertextuality, Biller's postwar German-Jewish literature also participates in this
anti-foundational polyphony.

The performative penchant for black humor and the grotesque in the
oeuvres of George Tabori, Edgar Hilsenrath, and other Germanophone

Jewish writers from the generation preceding Biller's corresponds as well to the "pop postmodernism" of Roth's work.[11] In the process, these writers also give the lie to the "impermissibility" of art after Auschwitz. The putative "unspeakableness" of the Holocaust, writes Michael André Bernstein, the seeming inability of language and other media "to engage it adequately, is precisely what constitutes much of the conversation about [it]."[12]

To be sure, Biller reflects repeatedly upon the inevitability of the "Shoah business," that peculiar circumstance that the Holocaust has "always already" been commodified in fiction. At least since Adorno's revisions to his dictum that "to write a poem after Auschwitz is barbaric," critics have been aware that the practice of art in post-Shoah culture both presupposes and reinscribes mass culture.[13] No child of camp survivors, Biller neither is nor wants to be understood as a performer of postmemory. Rather, his fiction has become decidedly de-essentializing since his debut collection of 1990, *The "Tempo" Years.*[14] Witness the recent controversy surrounding his *Esra* novel, comparable to the controversy surrounding *I Married a Communist*, Roth's recent novel which of all his work comes nearest to the category of *roman à clef.*[15]

For quite some time now, Biller has emphasized a postidentitarian irony as least as much as a putative solidarity or "identity politics." Yet, long prior to the *Esra* affair, critics had willingly overlooked the self-reflexive dimensions of Biller's work. Indeed, immediately following the partial censoring of *Esra*, Biller's "freedom of expression" was defended so insistently that reviews of his 2004 collection of stories, *Amber Days* (*Bernsteintage*), seemed exclusively mediated by it.[16] Since his first published stories, his (now) two decades-old *oeuvre* has been veritably obsessed with the undermining of conventional narration and the unsettling of artificial distinctions between "fact" and "fiction." In the end, what may be most compelling about Biller's prose fiction is the way it performs a consciousness of its own constructedness.[17] It enacts a subjectivity that seeks to acknowledge Jewish difference without fetishizing it, to represent ethnicity without having to be "representative." In the seemingly interminable struggles between irony and solidarity, irony seems to be ahead in Biller's work – at least at points.

II

Let us consider Biller's "Finkelstein's Fingers," which first appeared in 1994.[18] The complex and destabilizing narrative frame of the story renders it at first glance as self-perpetuating as a Möbius strip. At this stage of Biller's career, an increasingly metafictional trajectory had already been taking shape. Four of the sixteen stories in *Land der Väter und Verräter* (*Land of Fathers and Betrayers*) – where "Finkelstein's Fingers" first appeared in German – feature "Maxim Biller" as a character or protagonist. In "Finkelstein's Fingers," as elsewhere in Biller's fiction, the contingency of writing – and not just its commodification – is repeatedly the object of reflection. Upon traveling to New York to find an American publisher for his taboo-breaking, provocative stories about "Germans" and "Jews" after the Holocaust, a German-Jewish writer (yet another thinly disguised Billerian narrator) encounters on the street a non-Jewish German woman. Anita, a generation older than he, is in the midst of a midlife crisis, having abandoned her husband, family, and dog in Hamburg so as to study creative writing at Columbia University under the tutelage of a self-important American-Jewish writer, Sam Finkelstein. Although the possibilities for transference and countertransference are startling at first, they represent yet another moment in the story's unsettling of the notion of *author*, especially when Anita suggests that pseudo-Biller ghostwrite her semester project, a 3,000-word prose fiction on Miklós Radnóti for Finkelstein's seminar.

None of the three central players in "Finkelstein's Fingers" seems to grasp the identities, or the respective *authorships*, of the others. Their subject positions seem to overlap, even to be substitutable at times. The reader is presented with a story of three people caught up in the "German-Jewish symbiosis" – a symbiosis brought to bear by conventional, constraining normativities. These normativities in turn predate the Third Reich and the Holocaust. At stake in "Finkelstein's Fingers" are three individuals, unaware of the extent to which they are subjected – and *subjectified* – by norms. Particularly striking is the moment in which Anita and pseudo-Biller formulate their plan to write the story. After initial misunderstandings, Jewish German and non-Jewish German discover *the* topic which they have in common. Their meeting and this realization take place significantly *outside* of Germany, in the "semi-neutral" (to borrow Jacob Katz's term) space of the United States, specifically New York City as a site of potential "multi-culture."[19] At the formative moment when the topic is decided upon for Anita's assignment, Anita and pseudo-Biller utter in unison "'Ho-lo-caust'" (FF 155).

As issues of both narrative and cultural positionality are repeatedly foregrounded, the reader is confronted with not two, but *three Doppelgänger*: Finkelstein, Radnóti (the historically authentic Hungarian-Jewish "Holocaust" poet), and a first-person narrator who is biographically proximate to Biller; hence my designation "pseudo-Biller." As a result, the split of individual and double, private and normative subjectivity is thematized from the first lines of "Finkelstein's Fingers":

> We sat with our backs to the street, on wide comfortable leather stools, and there was a mirror hanging over the bar. In the mirror, you could see Broadway which down here…felt as cold and evil as a dark forgotten space (FF 149).[20]

At the end of the first section (FF 151), however, in that same mirror, Biller's narrator sees for the first time Finkelstein, who, he notes, "resembles" him.

The central representation (indeed the *Falke*) in this novella is the photograph that Anita shows the narrator.[21] Instead of being a portrait of the murdered writer Radnóti, it turns out to have been a photo of Finkelstein. Radnóti, for his part, propels Anita's attachment to his "doubles" – an attachment that results in a sexual union with pseudo-Biller in the framework of the narrative. This in turn points forward to the implied sexual symbiosis of Anita and Finkelstein. Anita is at the center of this triangle, as she is ultimately placed (by Biller) in the subject position of the author, thus unsettling the putatively negative symbiosis of "German" and "Jew." Not only does she seduce Finkelstein, the perlocutionary protagonist of her story, but she and the apparent co-author (whose own work is rejected in the story by American literary agents) have the last laugh on Finkelstein: the story, "Finkelstein's Fingers," was in fact first published in English, becoming as well the basis for the first theatrical rendering of Biller's fiction to be performed on an English-language stage.[22]

Indeed, sexual relations between Anita and Jewish writers of divergent background become a trope in the story, an occasion for ironic self-reflexion as well as commodification. When Anita recognizes Biller's semi-autobiographical narrator on the street in New York City, she addresses him immediately in German, comparing his face to that of the "Hungarian" Radnóti: "Then she said, as directly as at the start, that I didn't deserve Radnóti's eyes or face, that I, a child of prosperity, didn't know at all what was really important in life and literature" (FF 150). Attempting to impress him with her maturity and worldly wisdom is her transparent method of seduction. At the same time, she repeatedly evacuates the distinction of literary and non-literary. As the ultimate narrator (of the primary narrative), Anita proves more performative than could be imagined. In the end, she facilitates through her assigned story *her* seduction of Finkelstein, while at the same time repeatedly destabilizing stereotypes of "German" and "Jew."

When Anita claims that "in the end you can change anything you want: your professor, your history, your father, your mother, and even the country you're from" (FF 153), it is a claim against positionality and normativity. It also foreshadows the ultimate undermining of narrator and narration in "Finkelstein's Fingers." The same undermining is anticipated when the narrator, in this anticlimax, responds with "What do you actually want from me?" (FF 153). He feels he can no longer understand, much less re-read, the taboo-breaking stories he had written six months earlier in Germany: "I glided across the words and sentences as if they were merely pretty geometric patterns and lines" (FF 154).[23] This reference to a geometric narrative pattern may indicate that Biller, characterized by some as "arrogant," had endeavored to incorporate some of the earliest criticisms of his reviewers. More importantly, what is signaled is that the apparently sedimented normativities of the "German" and "Jew" are subject to being undermined.

In the concluding narrative irony, the ultimate object of transference, the famous writer Finkelstein, does not comprehend that the story just told – the story submitted to him as Anita's semester project – is a fiction about "Jews" and "Germans." Nor does he grasp its gestures toward undoubling and destabilization, mistakenly referring in his evaluation of Anita's story to the "mad garden of your character-multiplying machine" (FF 164). The magisterial Finkelstein, who claims always to know "what to expect," fails here to reflect upon his own projections and transferences. Despite the circumstance that *he* opts for a form of repetitive acting out, the narrative of "Finkelstein's Fingers" and its actors do not follow him in foreclosing other subject positions. For "the very possibility of identification," as Butler explains, "depends on a reiteration that is in no sense determined fully in advance."[24]

III

This theory of normative citationality, that "norms are actively lived and reworked at the very moment of their embodiment," permits a reading of "Finkelstein's Fingers" as an *embodying* narrative.[25] In each instance, seemingly insignificant norms are cited and performed, but their contingency is revealed, putting the lie to the necessity of their iterability. The anticipated "last word" of the novella is ironically put in the mouth not of Anita or the Biller figure, but of Finkelstein: "Who of us really knows if what we write is really true?" (FF 165).[26]

Such self-reflexive fictions, like (truly performative) speech acts, imply that it is possible to unsettle seemingly intransigent norms.[27] In elaborating her theory of performativity, Butler writes – and here one might wish to substitute "ethnicity" for "gender" – that "a reiterated enactment of norms... produce[s], retroactively, the appearance of gender as an abiding interior depth."[28] Even though gender is constituted performatively, "through a repetition of acts (which are themselves the encoded action of norms)," it is not therefore predetermined.[29] In an intensification of this formulation, Butler contends that "gender might be remade and restaged through the reiterative necessity by which it is constituted....[G]ender does not represent an interior depth, but produces that interiority and depth performatively as an effect of its own operation."[30] This means that systems of domination are not totalizing, but rather "hegemonic forms of power that expose their own frailty in the very operation of their iterability."[31] Likewise, in Biller's "Finkelstein's Fingers," antisemitism as enacted by non-Jews *and* Jews is simultaneously deconstructed as a reiterated performance. And in Biller's *Esra*, "anti-Armenianism" as practiced by a Turkish national of (possibly) Jewish descent is at the ideological/political center of the novel. It is the precise reason, in a paradigmatic example of projection and counter-projection, why Esra's mother rejects and despises Adam. He is of partial Jewish and Armenian descent, and she, despite her liberalism and putative

Jewish descent, fails to acknowledge Turkish complicity in the 1915–17 genocide of Armenians.

As performances, then, antisemitism and anti-Armenianism are revealed to be lacking in "interior depth" as well as performative force. Such interiority is, *pace* Butler, only an *effect* of previous operations of a highly contingent citationality. This citationality retroactively produces a certain normative "Jewishness" (or "Germanness"), but "the term that claims to represent a prior reality produces retroactively that priority" – as yet another effect of its own operation.[32]

This enables an instructive reading of the 1990 novella "Harlem Holocaust," discussed (almost without exception) in every analysis of Biller's *oeuvre* but seldom indicated as a predecessor to "Finkelstein's Fingers." The only longer fiction of Biller's to have been republished in a new edition, "Harlem Holocaust" has been accurately construed as "a hall of mirrors" that "blurs fact and fiction," in the process entrapping the reader in an "insoluble dilemma."[33] In Biller's first full-scale novel, *The Daughter* (*Die Tochter*), unreliable narrators and narrative frames also predominate. Events recounted earlier in the 425-page novel are ultimately revealed to have been deceptive fictions.

Such a performativity-centered approach has been missing from the multiple interpretations of "Harlem Holocaust," and the significantly less frequent ones of *The Daughter*, even though many critics find Butler's work to be as useful for literary as for philosophical analysis. Another useful term that Butler deploys for theorizing the retroactive "depth effects" of identification is *sedimentation*. This formulation (the opposite, as it were, of "unsettling") has the advantage of encompassing the palimpsest effects of mirroring, doubling, and other modes of repetition thematized in "Finkelstein's Fingers" and elsewhere in Biller's fiction. To turn once more to Butler, what *matters* is what *settles*. That is, the realistic embodiment of social identities is created through time as "a sedimented effect of a reiterative or ritual practice."[34] Such practices produce the naturalizing, reifying effect of essentializing identities – gender, ethnic, and otherwise.

The doer, much like the deed, is also the embodied effect of *subjectification*. The doer is that which inhabits the norm, which for Butler has no exterior existence "outside" the subject. Rather,

> inhabitation is an action by which the norm itself is *reconstituted* in regulatory ideality. In other words, a person does not simply inhabit or approximate an existing set of norms, but the very action of inhabitation is what revivifies the norm, either reinstituting the norm or altering it in some way.[35]

Biller re-enacts a similar "inhabitation" in his essay "Holy Holocaust," which appeared in *Die Zeit* in 1996. In the precise moment of composing the piece, Biller describes how

[p]hrases like "mourning work," "coming to terms with the past" and "never again" crowded into my head without my having thought them myself. They are, in fact, not my words; they come from outside, from editorials and eulogies, from television speeches and welcoming addresses; they are phrases which I've meanwhile heard in my life more often than "please" and "thank you."[36]

But while writing about such speech acts, Biller goes on to conclude that these are "[p]hrases that are said each time in such a serious and touching way that I – and this is the worst thing about them– still have to believe in them."[37] In a later programmatic essay, the otherwise cynically inclined Biller privileges a "metaphysical hope."[38] This comment, seldom taken at face value by critics, is borne out in Biller's recent fiction (such as *Esra*) centered as it is upon romance.[39]

What Biller instantiates in the long quotation above is how a certain active doing and repeating characterize the subject prior to its stabilization. Inasmuch as subjects are themselves "practices" or "performances," processes that both sanction and foreclose certain norms, they are sedimented legacies of normatizations. Whereas de-normatization is clearly an impossibility, the *desedimentation* of enactments (e.g., subjectification) is not. It is thus the contribution of Biller's writing to foreground the contingent and constructed quality of "German" cultural norms, up to and including contemporary norms of "realist" fiction.

In this sense, the controversy surrounding *Esra* was already foreshadowed in "Finkelstein's Fingers," ten years earlier. The anti-feminism of many of Biller's protagonists doubtless added to his current bout of legal "German trouble." Yet, just as Butler emphasizes (after *Gender Trouble*) that those bodies rendered "ethnic" have been constituted discursively, one may locate in Biller's more recent *oeuvre* reflections upon the contingency of *gender* performativity. In *Esra*, the Billerian narrator writes of his mirror reflection: "[W]henever I look at myself I see the friendly cold face of my mother. I see her round eyes and in them this – I'm not sure how to put it – rather feminine expression of a person who is as a matter of principle mistrustful."[40]

IV

In "Finkelstein's Fingers," positionality and subjectivity are continually subject to reconstitution. A limited form of agency is made possible as performative language attempts to unsettle a deterministic hegemony. Lest we conclude that Biller's self-reflexivity here and elsewhere is merely a gesture, a contrarian anti-foundationalism (or pop-postmodernism à la Roth), we should ask (following Butler): "[H]ow do we read the agency of the subject when its demand for cultural and psychic and political survival makes itself known as *style*? What sorts of style signal the crisis of survival?[41] To "survive" at all as an embodied Jewish subject in present-day Germany seems to demand a coming to terms, a *working through*, at least on the level of discourse. Biller has suggested, especially in the wake of the *Esra* controversy, that he could *not* survive at all were it *not* for being able to write.

Yet Biller's work from "Finkelstein's Fingers" to *The Daughter* and *Esra* does not exemplify a Holocaust-inflected "traumatic realism."[42] Rather, his fictions at various moments unsettle constraining norms of Germanness and Jewishness. In the process, they represent a different type of destabilization. As performative writing that draws our attention to its own constructedness, Biller's fictions may yet be able to unsettle the post-Shoah narrative of dystopic cynicism that so extensively characterizes German-Jewish relations after 1945.

To be sure, the utopia of love proposed in *Esra* does not succeed. And perhaps it *cannot* succeed. In the first paragraph of the novel, the first-person pseudo-Billerian narrator already asks explicitly (and in a rather "performative" vein) just which of the characters involved will be responsible for the failure of the romance depicted. It is intimated that the responsibility is to be shared: "[W]ho will be to blame?" Nonetheless, by the close of *Esra*, a clearly outlined contingency has been revealed, and the reader discovers the processes that account for the unsuccessful symbiosis.

Upon first examination, Biller's writing and that of other contemporary Jewish Germans instantiate a much rehearsed debate about the commercialization of the Holocaust. Because he is an author who has for years reflected on this instrumentalization, it comes as no surprise that Biller also thematizes the process of instrumentalizing *kitsch*. That thin line in *kitsch* between sentimentality and cynicism is acknowledged in *Esra* as well: "I was embarrassing to *myself*, to have been so sentimental. Nothing is more senseless than Jewish kitsch – and nothing is more disappointing than the insight that you've fallen for it again." What is enacted by and through *Esra* has a less skeptical trajectory than expected. Indeed, it sounds almost credible when (the authentic) Maxim Biller wrote in an (all too authentic) *apologia* for himself and his fictions after *Esra* was first censored: "My intention was to tell a great, beautiful and tragic love story, as they have been told by the hundreds in the history of literature since [Heine's] *Book of Songs*."[43]

For all of Biller's attempts to demythologize the putative Jewish-German symbiosis, he refigures in *Esra* a narrative of *internal*, i.e., Eastern Jewish–Western Jewish, symbiosis. This objective is to some extent shared by *Moral Stories* (*Moralische Geschichten*, 2005), which are framed by the satirical love story of the (Jewishly *named*) couple Dudi and Shoshi.[44] In addition, he contends in a recent interview: "Perhaps with *Moral Stories* I'm ultimately having an impact on something....Perhaps with *Moral Stories* I can make the Germans loosen up in their relationship to Jews."[45]

Biller may also have "loosened up" himself somewhat. He thereby exemplifies the latest manifestation of German-Jewish popular culture. The question remains, however, precisely how Jews might "loosen up" when approaching Germans in the era subsequent to the *Schoah* – the newly Germanized term for *Sho'ah*. Biller's fictions, from "Harlem Holocaust" and "Finkelstein's Fingers" on through to *Esra* and *Moral Stories*, repeatedly perform the German-Jewish symbiosis in ways that draw attention to the constructedness of the post-Shoah *negative* symbiosis. And inasmuch as Biller, in both his fiction and his non-fiction, has openly fantasized about emigrating, it is noteworthy that he continues to live, write, and make headlines in Germany for the foreseeable future.

NOTES

Introduction

1 Zischler (1996).
2 Kafka (1994a: 171). Also cited in Kafka (1953: 348).
3 Kafka to Max Brod, November 5, 1923, in Kafka (1975: 464); my emphasis.
4 Anderson (2001: B7). Arguably a "man about town," Kafka was also an ironic observer of his contemporaries. In a new biography by Peter-André Alt (2005), Kafka is acknowledged as the *flâneur*, voyeur, reader of pulp fiction, and connoisseur of nightlife (including bordellos) which he truly was.
5 See Bernstein (1994).
6 Lyotard (1983: para. 93).
7 Stern (1975: 79–83).
8 Elon (2002: 12).
9 Hall (2000: 284–85).
10 Ibid.
11 On *Selbstwehr*, see particularly Jaeger (2005: 151–207).
12 Jonathan Elmer (1995: 31) comments that "responsible attempts to think historically are not achieved through allergic reactions to abstraction, to theoretical work or the fascinations of form; but rather, that history is known – only partially, of course, but irreducibly – *as form*, as the crystallized and sedimented figures of past imaginations."
13 One might wish to distinguish between the politics of identity and the more common term, "identity politics." Political theorist Wendy Brown (1995: 53) writes: "Even as it is being articulated, circulated, and lately institutionalized in a host of legal, political, and cultural practices, identity is unraveling – metaphysically, culturally, geopolitically, and historically – as rapidly as it is being produced."
14 Azade Seyhan (1996: 415) has shown how American Germanics has tended to resist the theoretical debates since the late 1970s around poststructuralism.
15 For a critique of *anti*-essentialism, see Gilroy, (1993: 102). Gilroy privileges a postmodern hybridity as a "chaotic, living, disorganic formation" which provides "no ground to the suggestion that cultural fusion involves betrayal, loss, corruption, or dilution"; Ibid. (122 and 144).
16 Culler (1992: 222).
17 Butler (1993: 22).

18 Butler (1990: 147). Put differently, the "production of an 'outside,' a domain of intelligible effects...unsettles the foreclosures which we prematurely call 'identities'", Butler (1993: 22). On the relationship between Foucault's work and psychoanalysis, Butler argues that "[t]here may be a way to subject psychoanalysis to a Foucauldian redescription even as Foucault himself refused that possibility"; Butler (1993: 23). Stuart Hall (1996: 15) confirms that the "centering of the question of identification, together with the problematic of the subject which 'assumes a sex,' opens up a critical and reflexive dialogue in Butler's work between Foucault and psychoanalysis which is enormously productive."

19 Adorno and Horkheimer (1947). The 1944 edition appeared in mimeograph and was circulated only to a handful of associates.

20 Adorno and Horkheimer (1972: 167).

21 See, for instance, Hohendahl (1989: 309–11). For a more generous reading of Adorno and Horkheimer, see Levin (1991). Levin argues that Adorno interprets the artwork in the age of its technological reproducibility simultaneously as a manifestation of alienation and as a "cipher of utopia."

22 Similar deficits can be found in the work of postwar *Judaics* scholars, some of whom were also newly (or previously) exiled Jewish Germans. Indeed, the field of Jewish Studies continues to be focused on intellectual and political history at the expense of the history of mass culture, studies of which have been almost entirely limited to post-1945 America. The work of S. Whitfield (1999) is the exception that proves this rule.

23 This interpretation of *Bildung* ("cultivation" or "formation") is most often associated with George Mosse (1985). Works by the revisionists include Rabinbach (1985: 78–124); and Aschheim (1996: 125–40). Cf. as well Derrida's (1990: 919–1045) problematic essay.

24 Adorno (1996: 360) himself later warned against precisely such pessimistic stock-taking: "Those who make a plea to preserve a radically guilty and shabby culture set themselves up as co-conspirators, while those who deny themselves this culture promote the very barbarity that culture has revealed itself to be"; my translation.

25 Adorno (1991: 83). Schmidt (1998: 835) highlights the importance of the announced sequel to *Dialectic of Enlightenment*: "The unwritten *Rettung der Aufklärung* [Rescue of Enlightenment] would awaken the enlightenment from its nightmare, restore it to consciousness, and set it back on its path." In addition, see Geoffrey Hartman's (1997: 123) analysis, which quotes Leo Löwenthal as saying that

> the leitmotif of Adorno's life and work was *"nit mitmachen"*: Don't collaborate, Don't play their game. This wariness was a deeply reasoned philosophic and social project that hoped to free the human subject from subjection.

26 Adorno and Horkheimer were not atypical, for it was often the most highly acculturated German Jews who managed to become American academics. This fact is not surprising if one considers that "[o]nly eighteen percent of gainfully employed refugees arriving near World War II were professionals, and many of these were doctors and lawyers rather than intellectuals"(Lowenstein 1989: 23).

27 Carey (1992). By the same token, then, one can argue that "high culture" is essentially a mass or middlebrow culture legitimated for (and usually *by*) social elites. See also Levine (1990). The relationship between the middlebrow and postmodernism is delineated by (Jewish American) critic Leslie Fiedler (1969: 151, 230, 252–54, 256–58) in his seminal essay. Fiedler had already declared in the 1950s that contemporary American literature was a Jewish *and* middle-class affair,

associating Saul Bellow with "highbrow" literature, J. D. Salinger with "upper middlebrow," Irwin Shaw with "middle middlebrow," and Herman Wouk with "lower middlebrow."

28 B. O. Peterson (personal communication, April 3, 1997); see also Peterson (2005).
29 Adorno often preferred what might be termed "lose–lose" dialectics; on this, see Berman (1999: 173–74).
30 Hansen (1993: xxxvi).
31 Hansen (1991: 3).
32 Bobo (1995: 3); cited in Miller, Govil, McMurria, and Maxwell (2001: 176).
33 Even though Scholem rarely missed an opportunity to expose what he viewed as the "indignities, illusions, and contortions" of German-Jewish assimilation, he confessed to Adorno in June 1939 that "the strangest and most alluring thing is the fact that the most original products of Jewish thinking are, as it were, products of assimilation"; quoted in Aschheim (2004: 915 and 928–29).
34 Bathrick (1992: 321).
35 Elmer (1995: 30–31).
36 S. Frith quoted in Elmer (1995: 6).
37 Felski (1999: B7). Felski summarizes what is a consensus among specialists:

> Cultural Studies...originated in the 1960s at Birmingham University's Center for Contemporary Cultural Studies, in England, and has since spread around much of the globe. It has a particular history, a body of canonical – though often contested – scholarly works, and an eclectic but distinctive set of concerns.... Until recently, when people talked about cultural studies, that field of study is what they meant.

38 Felski (1999: B7).

1 Between high and low, laughter and tears

1 "Bedenkt man aber, daß das Lachen, das Träne-Lachen aus höheren Gründen, das Beste ist, was wir haben [...], so wird man mit mir geneigt sein, Kafkas liebevolle Fixierungen zum Lesenswertesten zu rechnen, was die Weltliteratur hervorgebracht hat"; quoted in Wagenbach (1964: 144).
2 This thesis is recapitulated in recent work as well; see Elon (2002). On the terms "acculturation" and "assimilation," see Sorkin (1990: 27–33). Recent researchers prefer "acculturation," owing to the negative connotations of "assimilation," which many Zionists have used as a term of opprobrium. According to the sociologist Milton Gordon, assimilation is a continuum. Beginning with what he calls "acculturation," a type of "cultural assimilation," an ethnic group adopts the dress, recreational tastes, economic patterns, language, cultural baggage, and political views of the general society without necessarily losing its sense of group identity. Total assimilation and group disappearance, however, does not take place unless primary contacts – friendships, associations, marriage, and family ties – have disappeared. This "structural assimilation" and the final stage of "marital assimilation" render the minority indistinguishable from the culture at large (Gordon 1964).
3 "Western Jewish" and "Eastern Jewish" refer to cultures and cultural tendencies, for what is "Eastern Jewish" and what is "Western Jewish" cannot always be demarcated geographically. On the history of the term *Ostjude* to refer to East European Jews, see Aschheim (1982: 257, fn. 1) and Maurer (1986: 12–13). Aschheim and Maurer maintain that the term did not achieve popular currency until 1910. But even though the term first became widespread in connection with

the German occupation of Poland in World War I and the related ideas of an *Ostjudenfrage* (Eastern Jewish question) and an *Ostjudengefahr* (Eastern Jewish danger), the ideology of the *Ostjude* was thoroughly developed by the mid-nineteenth century, and it appears that the term was generally understood in pre-1900 Germany. In spite of its pejorative connotations, *Ostjude* and *Ostjüdin* will be used neutrally throughout this book in order to make a distinction between East European and West European Jewish life and culture.

4 On the "revenge of the *Ostjuden*," see Wertheimer (1988: 422).

5 See, for example, Gilman (1985, 1986).

6 Gilman (1986: 1–5).

7 Wertheimer (1987: 149).

8 This method is especially important, inasmuch as "[e]ine systematische Untersuchung der populären Berliner Unterhaltungsbühnen, der kulturellen Infrastruktur innerhalb der ostjüdischen Emigration und ihrer Beziehungen zueinander steht noch aus" (Riss 2000: 68).

9 The present study uses the term "ethnic" as it is commonly understood in America with reference to "ethnic groups" and related semantic fields.

10 Winz arrived in Berlin from Russia in the early 1890s. Unlike many other Eastern Jewish students at the Friedrich-Wilhelm-Universität, he concentrated on the humanities. On the Eastern Jewish student milieu in the Prussian capital at the turn of the century, see Bertz (1995: 149–54).

11 For an introduction to Winz and *Ost und West*, see D. Brenner (1998).

12 Wertheimer may be correct in claiming that Eastern Jews formed few public or political organizations, instead preferring synagogue associations and *Gemeinde* activities. At the same time, he may be too categorical when denying that the foreigners created cultural institutions of their own; see Wertheimer (1987: 179–80.

13 I would argue that reception of a text ultimately renders it "Jewish," more so than its producers or framework of production.

14 Schach (1901a: columns 179–90).

15 Despite his praise of (Eastern) Yiddish, Schach valorizes a set of theses that are questionable according to the present state of research on Yiddish.

16 "Der Jude ist eine Kampfnatur, er redet und denkt dramatisch....Kein Volk kann so charakteristisch mit den Augen und Fingern sprechen" (Schach 1901b: columns 351–52) All translations from the German in this chapter are my own.

17 "Man darf bei den Kunstanfängen einer in der ästhetischen Erziehung zurückgebliebenen Bevölkerung nicht den Maßstab der Lessing'schen Hamburgischen Dramaturgie anlegen....Die Judenheit Rußlands bedarf des jüdischen Theaters um kulturell und ästhetisch zu gesunden....Gerade das Schlichte, das Schöne und Natürliche begreift der russische Jude nicht, weil er durch Generationen pilpulistisch erzogen wurde und sich daran gewöhnte, sich mehr an Talmudathletik als an Blumen und Strahlen zu ergötzen. Die Seele des russischen Juden ist krank, vielleicht noch kränker als sein Körper" (Schach 1901b: columns 351, 356, 357–58). Schach and other leading writers of *Ost und West* hoped to persuade middle-class (especially female) Western Jews to identify positively with Eastern Jews depicted as downtrodden (and male); see D. Brenner (1998).

18 Quoted in Bercovici (1998: 79, emphasis added).

19 For a recent exploration of the work of singer–songwriter and Yiddish parodist, Mickey Katz, see Kun (2005: 48–85).

20 Chametzky (2001: 963).

21 The original reads: "'Furcht vor den starken Emotionen', die die Darbietung auslöse, weil sie den Zuschauern die Verwandtschaft mit dieser Kultur deutlich

mache." Such was the diagnosis by a reader of the *Jüdische Rundschau* as to why "Zionists" were not attending the Yiddish theater around 1921; cited without footnote reference in Maurer (1986: 738).

22 For an instructive summary of Kafka's Yiddish song evening, see Stach (2002: 57–65).

23 Albert Memmi, *Portrait of a Jew*; cited in Kun (2005: 72).

24 The original reads: "[W]ie viel mehr Jargon Sie verstehen als Sie glauben" (Kafka 1993b: 188–93). The text is based on notes taken by Elsa Taussig.

25 On this and other films that Kafka saw, see Zischler (1996).

26 The Herrnfelds' slapstick clowning may be more than merely comparable with Ernst Lubitsch's earliest comedies, such as *Schuhpalast Pinkus* (1916). This comic cinema was not the unique creation of Lubitsch (as is often assumed) as the Herrnfelds also directed films in the same epoch, many of them now lost (Sprengel 1997: 97).

27 *Mauscheln* means literally "to speak like Moses."

28 Chametzky (2001: 963).

29 For more details, see Riss (2000: 35).

30 Hellmann (1925), quoted in Riss (2000: 35–36).

31 On "respectability," see Mosse (1985).

32 Abrahamsohn (1901: columns 619–22).

33 Ibid.

34 One very promising area for future research is the nascent film sector in Berlin's immigrant "Lower East Side," i.e., the *Scheunenviertel*. For the sociocultural locus of the Yiddish stage there was to be found in the same landscape with one of Europe's highest densities of cinemas and carnivals. Coterminous and culturally linked, such signifying practices have been denigrated throughout German and European performance history. See also Sprengel (1995) and M. Brenner (1996: 191–92).

35 Moses Schwarzfeld, 1877, quoted in Bercovici (1998: 71–72).

36 A. Goldfaden, quoted in Bercovici (1998: 68).

37 Bercovici (1998: 82–83).

38 The film industry functioned as "a Trojan horse that smuggled nonbourgeois and antibourgeois values and modes of representation into the minds and hearts of the middle classes" (Jelavich 2004: 249).

39 The founder of German cabaret, Ernst von Wolzogen (1855–1934), wrote in 1911 that the best comedies he had seen in the U.S. were in one of New York City's Yiddish theaters; see von Wolzogen (1911: n.p.); also cited in *The Nation*, 4 April, 1912, n.p.

40 Dalinger (1998: 54).

41 One such theater, called the "Freie Jüdische Volksbühne," was founded officially in 1919; see Marx (2001).

42 Sprengel (1997: 71–73); translation by author.

43 Sprengel (1997: 92).

44 P. Jelavich (personal communication, 2003). The use of dialect in popular American song is associated with Jewish composer (and son of a cantor), Irving Berlin.

45 Another reason why the "good" Jewish kitsch of the Herrnfelds (and later Ernst Lubitsch) attracted attention as "too Jewish" was the lack of a larger audience of Eastern Jews for Yiddish theater in Berlin. The situation in Vienna reveals a similar trajectory in the decades between 1880 and 1930. The early Yiddish ensembles did not only run afoul of the Viennese municipal authorities but also the Viennese "Israelite community," which feared anti-Semitic riots on the basis of Yiddish-only performance (Dalinger 1998: 44–45).

46 Steinlauf (1995: 51).

47 See Scholem (1980).

48 On Winz's other business ventures, both dubious and legitimate, see D. Brenner (1998) and Winz's Papers, Central Zionist Archives, Jerusalem.

49 Marline Otte has recently examined *Jargon* theatres in Wilhelmine Berlin as spaces that allowed for an unexpected blurring of Jewish–Gentile relations. Otte argues that *Jargon* theatre, such as the Herrnfelds', did not emerge from authentic Yiddish entertainment, but that it employed Jewish themes and accents "to consciously play on cultural differences, not religious or racial ones, which should place them into the trajectory of German *Volkstheater*" (Otte 2004: 254). See also Otte (2001: 121–46).

50 Cf. Kafka's comment that his fellow Jews in Prague knew "more Yiddish" than they thought (Kafka 1993b: 188–93).

51 "Die strenge Auslegung einzelner Bestimmungen des Theaterrechts durch die Zensurbehörde wirkt sich objektiv als Behinderung, z.T. sogar als Verhinderung einer jüdischen Theaterpraxis aus, deren genuine Strukturen – als Wandertheater, als Mischform von Musik-und Sprechtheater etc. – in einem unübersehbaren Spannungsverhältnis zu den in Preussen gültigen Regelungen für das Theaterwesen stehen. Und nicht nur gelegentlich stellt sich der Eindruck ein, daß dieser objektiv gegebene Konflikt von den zuständingen Beamten mit einer gewissen subjektiven Befriedigung ausgespielt und auf die Spitze getrieben wird" (Sprengel 1995: 39).

52 Döblin (1985: 385); quoted in Sprengel (1995: 30).

53 Sprengel (1995: 74).

54 "Er [the playwright Gordin] war für die Armen und gegen die Reichen. Für die Huren und gegen die feinen Damen. Für die Waisen und Bastarde und gegen die ehelich Gesicherten. Er war auch für mich" (Granach 1992: 219). Born in 1890 as "Isaiah Szaiko Gronach" in Werbiwici, Galicia (Austro-Hungary), Granach arrived in Berlin at the age of 16, after having appeared in the Yiddish traveling theater. In 1909, he was accepted into Max Reinhardt's *Schauspielschule*, the premier drama academy of its time.

55 See M. S. [Binjamin Segel] (1902: 847–52). This article is purportedly a description of the Gimpel Theater in Lemberg. For Granach's description of the performances, see Granach (1992: 219–27). Cf. Sprengel's discussion of the "Orientalische Operetten-Gesellschaft," also in Lemberg, to which Segel (himself a Lemberger) is likely referring (Sprengel 1995: 34–43).

56 Schach (1901b: column 356).

57 See the Leo Winz Papers, Central Zionist Archives, Jerusalem.

58 While David Pinski's drama, *Ayzik Sheftl*, is something of an anomaly in the history of Yiddish theater in Wilhelmine Germany, it was likely staged both in Yiddish and in German translation as early as 1905 (Sprengel 1995: 131–32, fn. 190). See also Pinski (1905). This volume was for many years the only translation of a Yiddish drama to be found on the list of its publisher, the Jüdischer Verlag.

59 "[Asch ist] bei weitem nicht der begabteste unter den jüdischen Dichtern…Seine Dichtungen haben Seele, aber keine tiefe und starke, Stimmungen, aber keine abgetönten, nüancierten, feinen, Rhythmus, aber einen eintönigen, wie das Summen einer Biene an einem Sommertag, Wahrheit, aber eine alltägliche, manchmal banale. Es gibt Gebiete der Kunst, die ihm unzugänglich sind, Winkel der Seele, die für ihn unsichtbar sind" (Coralnik 1907: columns 459–60).

60 German "Gefühlsstimmung, Seelenerguß, [and] Naturempfinden" (Meisels 1908: column 509).

61 See also Luba Kadison's recently published memoir of the Vilna Troupe and her life with Joseph Buloff (Kadison and Buloff (with I. Genn) 1992).

62 See Niger (1960).

63 *Ost und West* reported on what was perhaps the first *jungjüdischer Abend* organized by Buber in February 1902; for Buber's account, see his letter to Herzl of May 3, 1902 in Buber (1972: 173).

64 For a "public relations" portfolio on the folksong evenings, see "Urteile der Presse über die Jüdischen Volksliederabende," in *Ost und West*, December 1912, columns 1169–1200. For a negative, "purist" review, see Kaufmann (1919: 61); see also the positive review by Kaufmann's mentor (Birnbaum 1912: columns 17–24).

65 Winz's contract selling the opera rights to Ansky's *Dybbuk* is available in the Leo Winz Papers, Central Zionist Archives, Jerusalem.

66 For litigation concerning rights to Ansky's *Dybbuk*, see Winz's letter of justification to Rechtsanwalt Dr. Wenzel Goldbaum dated October 31, 1921: "Der verstorbene Anski [Ansky] war Mitarbeiter meiner Zeitschrift. Ich war der Erste und Einzige, der das europäische Publikum mit seinen Schriften bekannt gemacht hat. Gleich nach Erscheinen des 'Dibuk' schickte mir Anski ein Exemplar seines Werkes mit einer Widmung und richtete an mich die Bitte, für eine deutsche Übersetzung des Dramas, sowie für dessen Aufführung auf einer deutschen Bühne zu sorgen. Die darauf bezügliche Stelle seines Briefes lautet wörtlich, wie folgt: 'Ich bitte Sie, es zu lesen (das mir mit einer Widmung zugeschickte Exemplar) und wenn Sie es interessant genug finden, wäre ich Ihnen von tiefstem Herzen dankbar, wenn sie für die deutsche Übersetzung des Dramas, sowie für seine Aufführung auf einer deutschen Bühne sorgen wollten.' Da die Bitte des Autors wenige Tage vor seinem Tode an mich gerichtet war, so hielt ich mich ganz besonders für verpflichtet, seinen Wunsch zu erfüllen. Zunächst sorgte ich dafür, daß die jüdischen Schauspieler, die den 'Dibuk' in Rußland aufgeführt und berühmt gemacht haben, ihn auch dem Berliner Publikum in der Muttersprache der Helden des Stückes vorführen. Über den Umfang der materiellen Opfer, die ich für diesen Zweck uneigennützig gebracht habe, und noch fortwährend bringe, ist mein Freund, Herr Rechtsanwalt S. Gronemann, sowie die jüdischen Schauspieler und die Direktoren des Jüdischen Künstlertheaters orientiert. Aus den gleichen, ideellen Gründen habe ich, bald nach Erhalt des Briefes, einen meiner Mitarbeiter veranlaßt, den 'Dibuk' zu übersetzen. Der betreffende Herr mußte aber nach Wien übersiedeln und ich wollte im Interesse des Werkes keine Übersetzung ohne meine Kontrolle (als Fachmann auf dem Gebiete des Chassidismus und des Kabbalismus) herstellen lassen. Inzwischen mußte ich eine längere Reise nach dem Orient antreten und konnte erst nach meiner Rückkehr mit der Übersetzung beginnen, die von Arno Nadel unter meiner Assistenz besorgt worden ist"; Leo Winz Papers, Central Zionist Archives, Jerusalem. Alfred Nossig's wife, Rosa, had made a counterclaim for the rights to the German translation.

67 "[V]ielleicht der tatkräftige [*sic*] Freund und Fördererer der jüdischen Kunst auf allen Gebieten"; quoted in Winz's letter to Rechtsanwalt Dr. Wenzel Goldbaum, October 31, 1921, in the Leo Winz Papers, Central Zionist Archives, Jerusalem, file.

68 See the Leo Winz Papers, Central Zionist Archives, Jerusalem.

69 On Yiddish publishing in Berlin, see G. Levine (1997: 85–108).

70 Cf. Victor Klemperer, who argued that Winz and his associates treated Eastern Jews "more kindly" (Klemperer 1989: vol. II, p. 489).

71 According to Sammy Gronemann, Winz was a benefactor to many, from young painters and Russian dancers to boxers and diplomats' wives; see Gronemann (1948: 139).

72 On Buber and *Der Jude*, see Reinharz (1985: 183–85) and Friedman (1981: 60). The most obvious imitator of *Ost und West* was the Hungarian-Jewish art and cultural journal *Mült és jövö* (Budapest, 1912–44).

73 Scholem (1982: 47).
74 "Die Mitglieder des Vereins Bar-Kochba waren wegen des Namens des Stückes gekommen und mußten enttäuscht sein. Da ich Bar-Kochba nur aus diesem Stücke kenne, hätte ich keinen Verien so genannt" (Kafka 1990: vol. 1, pp. 196–97).
75 See Kafka's letter to Felice Bauer, November 3, 1912, in Kafka (1976: 75).
76 Kafka noted as well how the Yiddish actors were compelled to perform in a tawdry Prague nightclub, despised and insulted by the doorman (a notorious pimp and brothel-owner) and others for their amateurishness on stage.
77 See Kafka's letter to Felice Bauer of October 27, 1912, in Kafka (1976: 59).
78 "[D]ie Bewegung der Geister, das einheitliche Zusammenhalten des im äußeren Leben oft untätigen und immer sich zersplitternden nationalen Bewußtseins, der Stolz und der Rückhalt, den die Nation durch eine Literatur für sich und gegenüber der feindlichen Umwelt erhält, dieses Tagebuchführen einer Nation, das etwas ganz anderes ist als Geschichtsschreibung, und als Folge dessen eine schnellere und doch immer vielseitig überprüfte Entwicklung, die detaillierte Vergeistigung des großflächigen öffentlichen Lebens, die Bindung unzufriedener Elemente, die hier, wo Schaden nur durch Lässigkeit entstehen kann, sofort nützen, die durch das Getriebe der Zeitschriften sich bildende, immer auf das Ganze angewiesene Gliederung des Volkes [...] – alle diese Wirkungen können schon durch eine Literatur hervorgebracht werden, die sich in einer tatsächlich zwar nicht ungewöhnlichen Breite entwickelt, aber infolge des Mangels bedeutender Talente diesen Anschein hat" (Kafka 1983: entry of December 25, 1911, p. 151); emphasis added.
79 "Und schließlich merkt man...daß sie sich selber auslachen im bittern Ernst"; T. Lessing, "Jiddisches Theater in London", *Die Schaubühne*, vol. 6, nos 17 and 18, April 28, 1910 and May 5, 1910, p. 485; quoted in Sprengel (1995: 286). See also Lessing (1984).
80 "Wir schimpften erbarmunglos über die schlechten Stücke und das schlechte Spiel und gingen doch wieder hin" (Granach 1992: 208).
81 On the reinvented tradition of Yiddish theater in 1990s post-Wende Berlin, see Peck (2006).

2 "*Schlemiel*, Shlimazel"

1 Scholem (1976: 63–64).
2 For those who are not *au courant*, the difference between these complex Yiddish disparagements is as follows: a *schlemiel* is a person who spills her soup; a *schlimazel* is the one she spills it on. The *schlemiel* brings on her own misfortune, while it gets handed directly to the *schlimazel*. For a good recent overview of Cultural Zionism, see Bruce (2007).
3 In Herzl's *Altneuland*, Jewish immigrants to Palestine are also greeted positively by the main (Palestinian) Arab character, Reschid Bey.
4 "Briefe aus Neu-Neuland," *Schlemiel*, November 1903: 2.
5 In spite of its pejorative connotations in German, *Ostjude* will be used neutrally throughout this chapter in order to render a distinction between East European and West European Jewish life and culture.
6 For examples of this tradition of ideology critique, see Gilman (1982); and see Grimm and Hermand (1986).
7 Western Jews were enjoined to become "too Jewish" – if one may adapt this late twentieth-century Americanism to an early Zionist setting. On this phrase, see Kleeblatt (1996). This volume is based upon the exhibition of the same name, held at The Jewish Museum, New York, March 10–July 14, 1996.

8 There are many reasons to prefer the term "performance" to designate the "Letters from New-Newland" in *Schlemiel*; see the introductory and final chapters to this book.
9 Efron (1994: 3). On "Jewish Orientalism," see also Kalmar and Penslar (2005).
10 Efron (1994: 3).
11 Biale (1986: 11).
12 Arendt (1978: 70).
13 Gronemann (1948: 139).
14 *Schlemiel*, vol. 2, no. 2, April 1904: 33.
15 Boyarin and Boyarin (1993: 693–725).
16 Letter from Theodor Herzl to Max Jungmann, December 7, 1903. Herzl even funded anonymously a prize for the "best joke" on a monthly basis.
17 Luz (1988: 231).
18 Coupe (1985: xi).
19 On Winz generally and on his successful techniques at the *Gemeindeblatt*, see Brenner (1998: 54–56).
20 "Das Assimilantentum gibt eine so breite Fläche für eine humoristische Schilderung, dass es Ihnen am Stoff nicht fehle kann"; T. Herzl to Erwin Rosenberger, in Schäfer and Rubin (1996: 461–62).
21 The subtitle of Winz's production was "Jüdisches Blatt für Humor und Satire." Under Jungmann and Gronemann, the re-named *Schlemiel* appeared monthly from November 1903 to June 1905. In the next years, two special Purim issues were published, and the magazine experienced a short-lived post-World War I rebirth under Jungmann and Nathan Birnbaum's son, the artist Menachem Birnbaum.
22 Coupe (1985: xii).
23 Jungmann (1959: 62 f.); cf. Schäfer and Rubin (1996: 438, 445–46, 493).
24 See the files of Israel Auerbach, Central Zionist Archives, Record Group AK 102.
25 "Briefe aus Neu-Neuland," *Schlemiel*, November 1903: 2.
26 Gronemann, *Erinnerungen*, p. 140.
27 Ibid., December 1903, p. 11. The German reads: "O Gott, O Gott, ich hab' immer so Angst, dass er mal 'neinplumst.'"
28 Ibid., February 1904, p. 12.
29 Ibid., March 1904, p. 22.
30 For related discussions, see Mosse (1985) and Breines (1990).
31 "Briefe aus Neu-Neuland," *Schlemiel*, February 1904: 12.
32 One might argue that colonialism represented the more "normal" aspect of German nationalism, more oriented toward economic expansion and bourgeois values than settler-oriented *völkisch* ideologies were. For more on the complicated relationship between Nazism and colonialism, see Smith (1986). On the German colonies in Africa, consult Smith (1978), Gann and Duignan (1977), and Hull (2005).
33 See Wisse (1971).
34 Quoted in Nemitz (2002: 240).
35 Briefe aus Neu-Neuland," *Schlemiel* (Purim [Feb.] 1907): n.p.
36 Oring (1992: ix).
37 Ibid., p. 14. Oring's arguments implicitly address popular perceptions of "political correctness": "Humor depends upon the intellect for its creation and appreciation. Humor, first and foremost, appears to be a subspecies of play [...] Like aggression, play must be considered a primary impulse, an impulse *sui generis*, not reducible to more fundamental impulses. Despite occasional similarities in their surface behaviors, aggression and play are semiotically distinct: The playful nip denotes the bite, but it does not denote what would be denoted by the bite" (Oring 1992: 148).

38 Ibid., p. 202; emphasis added.
39 Ibid.
40 Zipes (1991: 134–35).
41 Gilman (1985: 23–24).
42 See in particular Reichl and Stein (2005).
43 Bhabha (1998: xviii). See also Bhabha's work on "mimicry," "hybridization," and "in-betweenness," especially in Bhabha (1994).
44 Hill (1993: 230). Hill also notes that the "challenging" character of Jewish wit has been elided from many treatments of the subject (see ibid.: 31–32).

3 A German-Jewish hermaphrodite

1 Body (1993: 8). This is a reprint of the original 1907 edition. Further references are to this edition with *Girl Years* and page numbers in parentheses. Further references to Simon's essay, "Wer war N. O. Body?" (167–246), are designated below as "Simon's essay." All translations from *Girl Years* and "Simon's essay" are my own. A translation into English has recently been published as Body (2005).
2 See Simon's essay, p. 195.
3 Martha Baer was also an innovator in youth education, the social hygiene movement, and related activities.
4 See Simon's essay, p. 212.
5 For a summary of the literature on self-hatred, see Gilman (1986).
6 The possibility of lesbianism is summarily dismissed on page 94 of *Girl Years*, although it has been intimated in the preceding pages.
7 *Girl Years* may have also appealed to the working classes.
8 Uricchio and Pearson (1992: 6–7).
9 Barbin (1980). The original French edition was titled *Herculine Barbin, dite Alexina B.* (1978).
10 Presbar, "Vorwort" to *Aus eines Mannes Mädchenjahren*, pp. 2–3. On Presber, see Simon's essay, pp. 183–87.
11 *Aus eines Mannes Mädchenjahren*, pp. i–ii. On playing with fire, a favorite metaphor of Baer's, see Simon's essay, p. 202.
12 See especially the discussion of the effects of horror fiction on the young Baer and his playmates in *Girl Years*, pp. 15–16.
13 Baer was flexible, able to play a variety of roles. As a writer, too, he defies easy categorization concerning genre and style, exhibiting a range extending from popular articles and political lectures to scientific papers and historical essays.
14 On Morgenstern, see also Brenner (1998: 112–16).
15 The statement, "This book is a book of truth," is also repeated on the final page of *Girl Years*, p. 158.
16 For a statement of N. O. Body's essentializing theses, see *Girl Years*, p. 110. Woman are, for N. O. Body, not inferior, but different ("nicht *minder*wertig, sondern *anders*wertig"). The difference, moreover, lies in the "method."
17 One may interpret the long episode devoted to the experiences of shopgirls as an attempt to appeal to this audience. Another such appeal to female middle-class readers is represented by the (likely) fictionalized travel accounts in Baer's memoir, particularly the trips to Norway and Turkey.
18 On the illustrator Bernhard, see Simon's essay, p. 192.
19 For an example of puritanical respectability, see *Girl Years*, p. 29 as well as Hirschfeld's "Nachwort," *Girl Years*, pp. 163–66. On respectability in nineteenth-century Europe, see Mosse (1985).

20 Hirschfeld's analysis here is based on a legal interpretation of the 1900 German *Bürgerliches Gesetzbuch* [Civil Law Code], according to which citizens could freely choose their gender. Even so, both N. O. Body and Hirschfeld assert pragmatically that *fin de siècle* hermaphrodites might best choose masculine identities.

21 See the advertising materials on the final pages of the Edition Hentrich reprint of *Girl Years*.

22 Merten (1994) avoids the Jewish dimensions of the memoir, as do others that appeared in the Federal Republic of Germany in 1994. See, for instance, Kugler (1994: 24) and Vida (1994).

23 For a noteworthy example of post-DDR "passing literature," see Sinakowski's (1991) narrative of being gay and an informer for the Stasi.

24 On Baer's own confusion regarding Chingachgook, see Body (1993: 39 and 47).

25 On masochism, see *Girl Years*, especially p. 85. Let me again emphasize that Baer's memoir is classifiable as "self-hating" *only if* we also understand self-hatred as a projection of racism onto a perceived inferior other: women, blacks, Native Americans. Thus, when N. O. Body states a need for German role models instead of Indians, this is only normal – all too normal – for Wilhelminian Jewry and all too dismissible in the post-Holocaust era as a tragic pathology for, in the ironic context of *Girl Years*, any diagnosis of self-hatred deserves a grain of salt.

26 White (1973).

27 Butler (1990).

28 Butler (1990: 99).

29 Butler (1990: 4).

30 Butler (1991: 29–30, fn. 9).

31 Bennett and Woollacott (1987: 56).

4 Franz's (folk)lore

1 Kafka (1990: 839).

2 In the original German, the text reads: "Ebensowenig Rettung vor Dir fand ich im Judentum. Hier wäre ja an sich Rettung denkbar gewesen, aber noch mehr, es wäre denkbar gewesen, daß wir uns beide im Judentum gefunden hätten oder daß wir gar von dort einig ausgegangen wären" (Kafka 1992: 37).

3 Kafka/Brod (1989: vol. 2, 360); my translation. Some commentators contend that Kafka appeared to have found it problematic that psychoanalysis was skeptical of all "beliefs," including religious ones.

4 Grözinger (1994: 12).

5 Anderson (1992: 211 and 216).

6 Scholem had said at one point that "[i]n order to understand the Kabbalah, one had to read Franz Kafka's writing first, particular *The Trial*" (Scholem 1981: 125). Among other works by the scholars mentioned, see Alter (1993: 86–99), Strauss (1986), Anderson (1996: 79–99), and Beck (1986: 343–88). For other relevant (if less scholarly) works, see Tiefenbrun (1973) and Jofen (1987).

7 Stach (2005: 423).

8 Eilberg-Schwartz (1994: 121).

9 Eilberg-Schwartz (1994: 137–38).

10 On Kafka's Judaic literacy, Robert Alter (1993: 90 and 93) contends: "I think it is reasonable to say that had Kafka lived a century or two earlier, had he grown up in a pious milieu with his schooling entirely in the classic Jewish curriculum of sacred texts, his qualities of mind would have made him an excellent Talmudist, a first-rate exegete, and a brilliant weaver of kabbalistic homilies." Kafka was also "[o]ne of the keenest readers of the Bible since the masters of the Midrash, and an intermittent or incipient student of later Jewish texts [...]."

11 Wolfson (1995).
12 Kafka's references to autoeroticism in his writings suggest that autoeroticism was nearly as problematic as homoeroticism in the cultural systems which Kafka addressed in his life and work.
13 Kafka (1994a: 171). Also cited in Kafka (1953: 348).
14 "Da ich nichts anderes bin als Litteratur und nichts anderes sein kann und will…"; Kafka (1990: vol. 1, p. 579; entry of August 21, 1913). See also the nearly identical terminology in the letter of August 14, 1913 to Felice Bauer; Kafka (1976: 444). On Kafka's formulation of writing as a form of prayer, Strauss (1986: 288) summarizes the scholarship, writing that "[i]t seems abundantly clear by now that the enigma of Kafka the writer is located at the point of intersection between his religious quest and the agony of writing; or better: how Kafka's spiritual journey becomes articulated as a literary odyssey."
15 See Anderson (1992). Rabbi Nachman spoke about his own "teachings without clothes," according to Martin Buber. Nachman further claimed that he would be diplomatic enough to "clothe them" at times; Buber (1956: 30). (N.B. Buber's original edition, *Die Geschichten des Rabbi Nachman*, was first published in 1906.)
16 In the original German, the text reads: "Und die Menschen gehn in Kleidern/ Schwankend auf dem Kies spazieren,/Unter diesem großen Himmel…." (Kafka 1993a: 54).
17 Anderson (1996: 96). Of Brod's abridgments, Anderson explains that "[i]ronically, what Brod left untouched were precisely these 'disgusting' heterosexual relations that Kafka repeatedly characterized as a violation of his identity […]" (ibid.: 96).
18 Ibid., p. 96.
19 Ibid., p. 89.
20 Eilberg-Schwartz (1994: 4).
21 Ibid., pp. 3–4.
22 Ibid., p. 77.
23 Ibid., p. 95.
24 Ibid., p. 96.
25 On the role of Noah in "The Judgment," compare Politzer (1962: 139).
26 "Gedanken an Freud natürlich"; Kafka (1990: vol. 1, 461; entry of September 23, 1912).
27 In the original German, the text reads:

"Nein!" rief der Vater, daß die Antwort an die Frage stieß, warf die Decke zurück mit einer Kraft, daß sie einen Augenblick im Fluge sich ganz entfaltete, und stand aufrecht im Bett. Nur eine Hand hielt er leicht an den Plafond. "Du wolltest mich zudecken, das weiß ich, mein Früchtchen, aber zugedeckt bin ich noch nicht. Und ist es auch die letzte Kraft, genug für dich, zuviel für dich."

In F. Kafka (1994b: vol. 1, 56). One may inquire whether the use of the term "fruit" is meant to recall the signal Jewish expression, "fruit of my loins" (from the Yiddish).
28 The original German text reads: "Wohl kenne ich deinen Freund. Er wäre ein Sohn nach meinem Herzen. Darum hast du ihn auch betrogen die ganzen Jahre lang"; Ibid.
29 The original German text reads: "Totenengel [hatten] eben die Seele eines zu dieser Zeit einer weitentfernten russischen Stadt verstorbenen Wunderrabbis zum Himmel begleitet"; Kafka (1990: vol. 1, 277; entry of November 29, 1911).
30 Kafka (1990: vol. 1, 540; entry of June 25, 1914). After the turning-point in "The Judgment," Georg fears that his father might "fall and shatter." One might read this as referring to the "originary" breaking of the vessels in Kabbalah or to Moses breaking the first set of tablets of the Law (the "Ten Commandments").

31 See Strassfeld (1985: 116).

32 It is incorrect of many commentators to assume that the father dies when he falls. Instead, the stylistic emphasis of "The Judgment" is on the bed and thus on the erotic symbolism. In fact, the possibility of his falling is alluded to many times prior to this. One might even ask whether Georg himself is even clothed at the story's close, as the cleaning lady feels compelled to cover her face when he passes her on the stairs.

33 The desire to be penetrated and its close connection to the problem of marriage/ sexuality is arguably present in Kafka's earliest writings such as "Wedding Preparations in the Country" ("Hochzeitsvorbereitungen auf dem Land").

34 Eilberg-Schwartz (1994: 163).

35 The decision of Zipporah, Moses' wife, to circumcise her son shows that "Israelite women are in danger of losing their men to God. But God will leave their husbands intact, if as mothers they condone the genital disfiguration of their sons and acknowledge that Israelite masculinity has been sacrificed to God" (ibid.: 161–62).

36 Ibid., pp. 173–75.

37 Ibid., p. 161.

38 Compare the reference in "Das Urteil" to the priest in Kiev who cut a broad bloody cross onto his flat hand; Kafka (1994b, vol. 1, 54).

39 The full quotation in German is: "Soll wegen dieses Kommandanten und seiner Frauen, die ihn beeinflussen, ein solches Lebenswerk – er zeigte auf die Maschine – zugrunde gehen?" (Kafka 1994b, vol. 1, 225).

40 Boyarin's critical project in numerous works has been to pinpoint the invention of Jewish "heterosexuality" in nineteenth-century Western Europe. In particular, he has expanded our understanding of Jewish cultural history by uncovering the decisive role of gender in the autobiographically inflected projects of Freud, Theodor Herzl (1860–1904), and Bertha Pappenheim (1859–1936). Breaking with the conventional understanding of Otto Weininger (1880–1903) as an anti-feminist, "self-hating Jew," Boyarin examines him as a thinker, the discursive practitioner of "Judaism as gender." See Boyarin (1997).

41 Eilberg-Schwartz (1994: 33).

42 Ibid.

43 In the words of Eilberg-Schwartz (1994: 54): "The important point is to see how Freud in his own writing about *Moses and Monotheism* is characterized by the same repression I have suggested is operating in his religious tradition. Because he could not or would not think about why the image/body of the father God had to be veiled, Freud did not face the issue of the son's erotic desires for the father."

44 The original German text reads: "Der Freund ist die Verbindung zwischen Vater und Sohn, er ist ihre größte Gemeinsamkeit. Allein bei seinem Fenster sitzend, wühlt Georg in diesem Gemeinsamen mit Wollust" (Kafka 1990: vol. 1, 491; entry of February 11, 1913).

45 Kafka (1976: 117). The extended quote reads: "[U]nd die Nächte können nicht lange genug sein für dieses äußerst wollüstige Geschäft."

46 In the original German, the text reads: "wie eine regelrechte Geburt mit Schmutz und Schleim bedeckt aus mir herausgekommen" (Kafka 1990: vol. 1, 491; entry of February 11, 1913).

47 Kafka (1994b: vol. 1, 171). Anderson (1996: 91) is correct (if oblique) in contending that, in this passage, "there is no realist narrative need for the mother to copulate with the father in full view of the children." One does not have to be a professional graphologist to perceive that this scene in "The Metamorphosis" was handwritten quickly (and excitedly?) by Kafka; see the handwritten manuscript (Kafka 2003).

48 Kafka (1992: 37).

49 Kafka/Brod (1989: 360).

50 Eilberg-Schwartz (1994: 42).

51 According to Anderson (1992: 192), Kafka's "Loosian ascesis involved not so much a break with aestheticism as a radicalization of its basic tenet: the fusion (and confusion) of life with art."

52 In the original German, the text reads: "Ich schreibe auch hier, sehr wenig allerdings, klage für mich auch; *so beten fromme Frauen*" (Kafka/Brod 1989: 108); emphasis added.

53 In the original German, the text reads: "Coitus als Bestrafung des Glückes des Beisammenseins. Möglichst asketisch leben, asketischer als ein Junggeselle, das ist die einzige Möglichkeit für mich, die Ehe zu ertragen. Aber sie?" (Kafka 1990: vol. 1, 574; entry of August 14, 1913).

54 Grözinger (1994: 81).

55 Ibid., p. 77.

56 In the original German, the text reads: "mithat nechiko [,] Tod durch den Kuß, nur den Frömmsten vorbehalten" (Kafka 1990: vol. 1, 366; entry of January 26, 1912).

57 Kafka (1975: 173; letter of September 28, 1917).

58 Buber's influence on the Prague Circle had already been secured with his 1909 lecture, "The Meaning of Judaism," which deeply touched Brod and "converted him to a passionate Zionism" (Mendes-Flohr 1991: 85).

59 Grözinger (1994: 13 and 218).

60 Buber (1956: 21).

61 Deutsch (2001: 208).

62 In the original German, the text reads: "Unterhosen sichtbar....Haar auf dem Nasenrücken. Mit Fell eingefaßter Kappe, die er immerfort hin und her rückt. Schmutzig und rein" (Kafka 1990: vol. 1, 752: entry of September 14, 1915).

63 Eilberg-Schwartz (199: 239).

64 Kafka (1990: vol. 1, 878; entry of January 16, 1922).

65 In the original German, the text reads: "[I]ch kann auch sagen 'Ansturm gegen die letzte irdische Grenze' undzwar Ansturm von unten, von den Menschen her und kann, da auch die nur ein Bild ist, es ersetzen durch das Bild des Ansturmes von oben, zu mir herab"; Ibid.

66 For a recent reading of *The Castle* as a (Zionist-preoccupied) narrative of assimilation, see Neumann (2005: 307–40). See also Strauss (1988).

67 "Ich habe das Negative meiner Zeit, die mir ja sehr nahe ist, die ich nie zu bekämpfen, sondern gewissermaßen zu vertreten das Recht habe, kräftig aufgenommen. An dem geringsten Positiven sowie an dem äußersten, zum Positiven umkippenden Negativen, hatte ich keinen ererbten Anteil. [...] Ich bin Ende oder Anfang" (Kafka 1993a: 97).

5 Pogrom in … Berlin

1 The joke probably derives from Lenin's adage that *German* revolutionaries would never occupy a railway station without first buying tickets.

2 Belgum (1993: 91–92).

3 Kaplan (1991: 11).

4 At least during the Wilhelmine era, "converts generally did not abandon Jewish familial and friendship networks, nor were they abandoned in return" (Kaplan 2005: 150). See also van Rahden (2000: 141–74).

5 All translations from the German are my own, unless otherwise noted. Further references to "Versöhnung" are cited with installment dates and page numbers in parentheses.

6 For an important discussion of stereotypes of Jewish male bodies, see Breines (1990).

7 Maurer (1991: 344–74).

8 See also Radway (1991).

9 Modleski (1982: 25).

10 D. Boyarin (personal communication, July 20, 1996).

11 To be sure, there was already a preference for internal Jewish marriage in (upper) middle-class circles, whereas Christian–Jewish marriages were more frequent in other milieus; see Meiring (1998).

12 On Dohm (1781), see especially Hess (2002).

13 According to Michael Brenner (1996: 46–47), "[t]he Jewish youth movement shared with its non-Jewish counterpart a general rejection of the bourgeois home, with the added incentive that the Jewish homes may have been even more bourgeois than those of many of their non-Jewish comrades." See also *Blau-Weiss Führer* (1917).

14 Fuss-Opet [sic] (1931: 4); Opet-Fuß (1933; 1934: supplement, n.p).

15 In a useful summary of the German-Jewish response to 1918, Ruth Gay (1993: 243–44) writes:

> The enemies of the Jews (and of the Republic) found welcome fodder in the results of the wartime census of Jews in the armed forces, released in 1919 by an unofficial, pseudonymous, anti-Semitic author, "Otto Armin." The statistics he offered, presumably reflecting the official count, supported the slander that Jews had hung back behind the lines. Anticipating such slander, a special consortium of Jewish organizations had set up a Committee for War Statistics at the beginning of the war. It worked under the direction of two highly placed statisticians: Jacob Segall, head of the Berlin Bureau for Statistics on Jews, and Heinrich Silbergleit, director of the Office of Statistics for the city of Berlin between 1906 and 1923. They released their results in 1922 and the facts were very different from the story in the Otto Armin report: among the 550,000 Jews of German nationality, 100,000 had served in the war, 80,000 at the front. And 12,000 had died for Germany. What is more, 35,000 Jewish soldiers had received medals, and 23,000 had been promoted – 2,000 of them, in fact, to officer's rank. The Reichsbund jüdischer Frontsoldaten...was founded in 1919 with the express purpose of documenting, and thus honoring, the Jewish war dead.

16 Anti-semitic right-wingers also made an attempt on the life of journalist Maximilian Harden, a convert to Protestantism, in 1922.

17 Speech by Golo Mann in 1966, quoted in Mosse and Paucker (1971: 49).

18 Golo Mann in *Encounter* (June 1952); cited in Elon (2002: 370).

19 Peukert (1993: 60).

20 Walter (1999: 151).

21 Presbar (1921: 30–31); quoted in Mendes-Flohr and Reinharz (1995: 514).

22 Large (2002: 140).

23 Ibid., p. 124.

24 Ibid., p. 125.

25 West (1988: 107–8).

26 In certain respects, Jonas, the father, is a "gentle" (as opposed to a "tough") Jew.

27 Many scholars have eschewed comparisons of Jewish authors and audiences with their non-Jewish counterparts.

28 It should be noted that, for all the sudden shifts and improbabilities of *feuilleton* fiction, there is often a high degree of close observation and milieu detail,

suggesting that composition and organization were not haphazard. Some practitioners maintain that it actually requires more discipline to write on an installment basis.

29 See Adorno and Horkheimer (1947).

30 Numerous debates in reception theory and reader response theory since the 1960s involve the problematic notion of the "implied reader"; for a summary, see Holub (1984). The implied audience can be teased out from the text by drawing on social histories that use analytical categories such as class, education, gender, age, ethnicity, and religion; on this, see Jarausch (1989: 427–43).

6 After the "Schoah"

1 Remmler (2002: 25).

2 See Scholem (1976: 61–64).

3 Remmler (2002: 25).

4 Freedman (2001: 545).

5 Butler and Laclau (1997: 4).

6 Butler (1993: 22).

7 On this, compare the final pages of Butler's new foreword to *Gender Trouble* in the second edition of 1999.

8 Butler (1999: 147).

9 Butler (1991: 29–30).

10 Roth (1993: 334 and 336).

11 For some of the most recent scholarship on contemporary German-Jewish writing, see the following: Gilman (1995), Gilman and Remmler (1994), Gilman and Zipes (1997), Herzog (1997: 1–17); Nolden (1995), Remmler (2002), Remmler and Morris (2002), and Steinecke (2002: 9–16).

12 Bernstein (1998: 8).

13 The original quote (embedded in its original context) is: "Kulturkritik findet sich der letzten Stufe der Dialektik von Kultur und Barbarei gegenüber: nach Auschwitz ein Gedicht zu schreiben, ist barbarisch, und das faßt auch die Erkenntnis an, die ausspricht, warum es unmöglich wird, heute Gedichte zu schreiben. Der absoluten Verdinglichung, die den Fortschritt des Geistes als eines ihrer Elemente voraussetzte und die ihn heute gänzlich aufzusaugen sich anschickt, ist der kritische Geist nicht gewachsen, solange er bei sich bleibt in selbstgenügsamer Kontemplation" (Adorno 1963: 26).

14 Biller (1991).

15 Biller (2003a).

16 Biller (2004). Consider the titles of reviews of *Bernsteintage* such as "Ein fast neuer Maxim Biller" in *Die Zeit* (Isenschmid 2004) and "Tolles Comeback" in *Die Tageszeitung*. In the *Neue Zürcher Zeitung*, the reviewer praised Biller's "stilistische Eleganz" and "Kunstverstand" in *Bernsteintage* (Schneider 2004).

17 For a similar view, see Chase (2001).

18 Biller (1994a: 149–65). "Finkelstein's Finger" is cited hereafter in the body of this text as "FF" with page numbers in parentheses; translations from German into English are my own.

19 On "America" as a central figure mediating between Germany and the United States in newer discourse on the German-Jewish "symbiosis," see Kniesche (2006: 337–64).

20 The original reads: "Wir saßen mit dem Rücken zur Straße, auf breiten, bequemen Lederhockern, und über der Bar hing ein Spiegel. Im Spiegel sah man den Broadway, der hier unten…so kalt und böse wirkte wie ein dunkler vergessener Raum" (FF 149).

21 For the original elaboration of the *Falkentheorie*, see Heyse (1871: 5–22).

22 See Biller (1994b).

23 The original reads: "Ich glitt über die Worte und Sätze, als handelte es sich bei ihnen nur um hübsche geometrische Muster und Linien" (FF 154).

24 Butler and Laclau (1997: 13).

25 Butler (1997: 517).

26 The original reads: "Wer von uns weiß schon, ob das, was wir schreiben, denn auch wirklich stimmt?"

27 Butler has generally seconded self-reflexivity in all forms of art; see, for instance, her chapter on the film *Paris is Burning* in Butler (1993).

28 Butler and Laclau (1997: 14).

29 Ibid.

30 Ibid.

31 Ibid.

32 Ibid.

33 The new edition is Biller (1998); Chase (2001: n.p.).

34 Butler (1993: 10).

35 Butler (1997: 515).

36 The original reads: "Worte wie 'Trauerarbeit,' 'Vergangenheitsbewältigung' und 'Nie wieder' sich in meinen Kopf drängen, ohne daß ich selbst sie gedacht habe. Es sind ja auch nicht meine Worte, sie kommen von draußen, aus Leitartikeln und Gedenkreden, aus Fernsehansprachen und Grussadressen, es sind Worte, die ich in meinem Leben inzwischen öfter gehört habe als 'danke' und ' bitte'" (Biller 1996).

37 The original reads: "Worte, die jedesmal so ernst und anrührend ausgesprochen werden, daß ich an sie – und das ist das Schlimmste an ihnen – auch noch glauben muß" (Biller 1996: n.p.).

38 Biller (2000a).

39 Biller's recent collection, *Liebe heute* [Love Today] is characterized in *The New Yorker* as an example of "sad optimism."

40 The original reads: "Wann auch immer ich mich inzwischen betrachte, sehe ich das freundliche, kalte Gesicht meiner Mutter. Ich sehe ihre runden Augen und in ihnen diesen, wie soll ich sagen, eher weiblichen Ausdruck eines Menschen, der aus Prinzip mißtrauisch ist" (Biller 2003a: 158).

41 Butler (2000: 36); emphasis added. For a useful defense of Butler's "style," see Bérubé (1997: B5).

42 On this term, see Rothberg (2000).

43 The original reads: "[M]eine Absicht war es, eine große, schöne und tragische Liebesgeschichte zu erzählen, wie es sie in der Literaturgeschichte seit dem Buch der Lieder zu Hunderten gibt" (Biller 2003b: n.p.).

44 Biller (2005a).

45 The original reads: "Vielleicht bewirke ich am Ende mit den *Moralischen Geschichten* auch etwas....Vielleicht kann ich mit den *Moralischen Geschichten* die Deutschen lockerer machen im Verhältnis zu den Juden" (Biller 2005b: n.p.).

BIBLIOGRAPHY

Abrahamsohn, I. "Sternensöhne," *Ost und West*, August 1901: columns 619–22.

Adorno, T. W. "Kulturkritik und Gesellschaft," in R. Tiedemann (ed.), *Prismen. Ohne Leitbild*, vol. 1 of *Kulturkritik und Gesellschaft*, Munich: dtv, 1963, pp. 7–26.

—— *Negative Dialektik. Jargon der Eigentlichkeit*, vol. 6 of *Gesammelte Schriften*, R. Tiedemann (ed.), Frankfurt a. M.: Suhrkamp, 1996.

—— "The Schema of Mass Culture," in T. W. Adorno, *The Culture Industry: Selected Essays in Mass Culture*, J. M. Bernstein (ed.), London: Routledge, 1991.

—— and M. Horkheimer "The Culture Industry: Enlightenment as Mass Deception," *Dialectic of the Enlightenment*, New York: Herder and Herder, 1972.

—— and M. Horkheimer *Dialektik der Aufklärung: Philosophische Fragmente*, Amsterdam: Querido, 1947.

Alt, P.-A. *Franz Kafka. Der ewige Sohn. Eine Biographie*, Munich: Beck, 2005.

Alter, R. "Kafka as Kabbalist," *Salmagundi* 98/99, Spring/Summer 1993: 86–99.

Anderson, M. M. "German Intellectuals, Jewish Victims: a Politically Correct Solidarity," *The Chronicle of Higher Education*, October 19, 2001: B7.

—— *Kafka's Clothes: Ornament and Aestheticism in the Habsburg Fin de Siècle*, New York: Oxford University Press, 1992.

—— "Kafka, Homosexuality and the Aesthetics of 'Male Culture,'" in R. Robertson and E. Timms (eds), *Gender and Politics in Austrian Fiction*, Edinburgh: Edinburgh University Press, 1996, pp. 79–99.

Arendt, H. *The Jew as Pariah: Jewish Identity and Politics in the Modern Age*, R. H. Feldman (ed.), New York: Grove, 1978.

Aschheim, S. E. *Brothers and Strangers: The East European Jew in German and German Jewish Consciousness, 1800–1923*, Madison, WI: University of Wisconsin Press, 1982.

—— "German Jews beyond *Bildung* and Liberalism: The Radical Jewish Revival in the Weimar Republic," in K. L. Berghahn (ed.), *The German-Jewish Dialogue Reconsidered: A Symposium in Honor of George L. Mosse*, New York: Peter Lang, 1996, pp. 125–40.

—— "The Metaphysical Psychologist: On the Life and Letters of Gershom Scholem," *Journal of Modern History*, 76, 2004: 903–33.

Auerbach, I. Papers. Central Zionist Archives, Record Group AK 102.

Barbin, H. *Being the Recently Discovered Memoirs of a Nineteenth Century French Hermaphrodite*, intro. M. Foucault, New York, Pantheon, 1980.

—— *Herculine Barbin, dite Alexina B.*, Paris: Gallimard, 1978.

Bathrick, D. "Cultural Studies," in J. Gibaldi (ed.), *Introduction to Scholarship in Modern Languages and Literatures*, 2nd edn, New York: Modern Language Association of America, 1992.

Beck, E. T. "Kafka's Triple Bind: Women, Jews and Sexuality," in A. Udoff (ed.), *Kafka's Contextuality*, Staten Island, NY: Gordian Press, and Baltimore, MD: Baltimore Hebrew College, 1986, pp. 343–88.

Belgum, K. "Domesticating the Reader: Women and 'Die Gartenlaube,'" *Women in German Yearbook*, 1993: 91–111.

Bennett, T. and J. Woollacott *Bond and Beyond: The Political Career of a Popular Hero*, London: Macmillan, 1987.

Bercovici, I. *O sută de ani de teatru evreiesc în România* (One hundred years of Jewish theater in Romania), 2nd rev. edn, Bucharest: Editura Integral, 1998. Available from http://en.wikipedia.org/wiki/Yiddish_theatre (accessed July 15, 2006).

Berman, R. A. "Cultural Studies and the Canon: Some Thoughts on Stefan George," in *Profession 1999*, New York: Modern Language Association of America, 1999.

Bernstein, M. A. *Foregone Conclusions: Against Apocalyptic History*, Berkeley, CA: University of California Press, 1994.

—— "Homage to the Extreme: The Shoah and the Rhetoric of Catastrophe," *Times Literary Supplement*, March 6, 1998: 6–8.

Bertz, I. "Politischer Zionismus und Jüdische Renaissance in Berlin vor 1914," in R. Rürup (ed.), *Jüdische Geschichte in Berlin. Essays und Studien*, Berlin: Edition Hentrich, 1995, pp. 149–54.

Bérubé, M. "A Few Clear Words in Favor of Obscurity," *The Chronicle of Higher Education*, February 21, 1997: B5.

Bhabha, H. K. "Joking Aside: The Idea of a Self-Critical Community," in B. Cheyette and L. Marcus (eds), *Modernity, Culture, and "the Jew,"* London: Polity Press, 1998.

—— *The Location of Culture*, London: Routledge, 1994.

Biale, D. *Power and Powerlessness in Jewish History*, New York: Schocken, 1986.

Biller, M. *Bernsteintage. Sechs neue Geschichten*, Köln: Kiepenheuer & Witsch, 2004.

—— *Esra. Roman*, 1st edn, Köln: Kiepenheuer & Witsch, 2003a.

—— "Feige das Land, schlapp die Literatur: Über die Schwierigkeiten beim Sagen der Wahrheit," *Die Zeit*, April 13, 2000a. Available from http://www.zeit.de (accessed February 16, 2004).

—— "Finkelstein's Finger," in E. Lappin (ed.), *Jewish Voices, German Words*, trans. K. Winston, North Haven, CT: Catbird Press, 1994b.

—— "Finkelsteins Finger," *Land der Väter und Verräter. Erzählungen*, Köln: Kiepenheuer & Witsch, 1994a, pp. 149–65.

—— *Harlem Holocaust. Kurzroman*, Köln: Kiepenheuer & Witsch, 1998.

—— "Heiliger Holocaust," *Die Zeit [Magazin]*, November 8, 1996. Available from http://www.zeit.de (accessed February 16, 1999).

—— "Interview" with M. Schubert and J. Buhre, *Planet Interview*, July 7, 2005b. Available from http://www.planet-interview.de (accessed February 1, 2007).

—— *Land der Väter und Verräter. Erzählungen*, Köln: Kiepenheuer & Witsch, 1994.

—— *Moralische Geschichten. Satirische Kurzgeschichten*, Köln: Kiepenheuer & Witsch, 2005a.

—— "Stellungnahme zum Prozess um *Esra*. Verfasst für das Landgericht München," *Die Tageszeitung*, March 21, 2003b. Available from http://www.taz.de (accessed February 1, 2007).

—— *Die Tempojahre. Reportagen und Erzählungen*, Munich: dtv, 1991.

—— *Die Tochter. Roman*, Köln: Kiepenheuer & Witsch, 2000.

—— *Wenn ich einmal reich und tot bin. Erzählungen*, Köln: Kiepenheuer & Witsch, 1990.

Birnbaum, N. (pseudonym "Matthias Acher"), "Auf dem Volksliederabend von 'Ost und West'," *Ost und West*, January 1912: columns 17–24.

Blau-Weiss Führer. Leitfaden für die Arbeit im jüdischen Wanderbund "Blau-Weiss," Berlin: Bundesleitung Blau-Weiss, 1917.

Bobo, J. *Black Women as Cultural Readers*, New York: Columbia University Press, 1995.

Body, N. O. [i.e., K. Baer], *Aus eines Mannes Mädchenjahren*, H. Simon (ed.), Berlin: Edition Hentrich, 1993.

—— *Memoirs of a Man's Maiden Years*, intro. S. L. Gilman, trans. D. Simon, Philadelphia, PA: University of Pennsylvania Press, 2005.

Boyarin, D. "Permissible marriages under *halakha*," E-mail (July 20, 1996).

—— *Unheroic Conduct: The Rise of Heterosexuality and the Invention of the Jewish Man*, Berkeley. CA: University of California Press, 1997.

—— and J. Boyarin, "Diaspora: Generation and the Ground of Jewish Identity," *Critical Inquiry*, 19, Summer 1993: 693–725.

Breines, P. *Tough Jews: Fantasies and the Moral Dilemma of American Jewry*, New York: Basic Books, 1990.

Brenner, D. *Marketing Identities: The Invention of Jewish Ethnicity*, Detroit, MI: Wayne State University Press, 1998.

Brenner, M. *The Renaissance of Jewish Culture in Weimar Germany*, New Haven, CT: Yale University Press, 1996.

Brown, W. *States of Injury: Power and Freedom in Late Modernity*, Princeton, NJ: Princeton University Press, 1995

Bruce, I. *Kafka and Cultural Zionism: Dates in Palestine*, Madison, WI: University of Wisconsin Press, 2007.

Buber, M. "Introduction," in M. Buber (ed.), *Tales of Rabbi Nachman*, trans. M. Friedman, New York: Horizon, 1956.

—— *Briefwechsel aus sieben Jahrzehnten*, G. Schaeder (ed.), Heidelberg: Gütersloher Verlagshaus, 1972.

Butler, J. "Agencies of Style for a Liminal Subject," in P. Gilroy, L. Grossberg and A. McRobbie (eds), *Without Guarantees: In Honour of Stuart Hall*, London: Verso, 2000.

—— *Bodies That Matter: On the Discursive Limits of "Sex,"* New York: Routledge, 1993.

—— *Gender Trouble: Feminism and the Subversion of Identity*, New York: Routledge, 1990.

—— *Gender Trouble: Feminism and the Subversion of Identity*, 2nd edn, New York: Routledge, 1999.

—— "Imitation and Gender Insubordination," in D. Fuss (ed.), *Inside/Out: Lesbian Theories, Gay Theories*, New York: Routledge, 1991.

—— *Psychic Life of Power: Theories in Subjection*, Stanford, CA: Stanford University Press, 1997.

—— and E. Laclau. "The Uses of Equality (Exchange of Letters between Judith Butler and Ernesto Laclau)," *Diacritics: A Review of Contemporary Criticism*, 27, Spring 1997: 3–12.

Carey, J. *The Intellectuals and the Masses: Pride and Prejudice Among The Literary Intelligentsia, 1880–1939*, Boston, MA: Faber and Faber, 1992.

Chametzky, J. "The Golden Age of the Broadway Song," in J. Chametzky, J. Felstiner, H. Flanzbaum, and K. Hellerstein (eds), *Jewish American Literature: A Norton Anthology*, New York: Norton, 2001.

Chase, J. "Shoa Business: Maxim Biller and the Problem of Contemporary German-Jewish Literature," *German Quarterly*, 74, Spring 2001: 111–32.

Coralnik, A. "Schalom Asch als Dramatiker," *Ost und West*, July 1907: columns 459–60.

Coupe, W. A. *German Political Satires from the Reformation to the Second World War*, White Plains, NY: Kraus, 1985.

Culler, J. "Literary Theory," in J. Gibaldi (ed.), *Introduction to Scholarship in Modern Languages and Literatures*, New York: Modern Language Association of America, 1992.

Dalinger, B. *Verloschene Sterne. Geschichte des jüdischen Theaters in Wien*, Wien: Picus Verlag, 1998.

Derrida, J. "Force of Law: The 'Mystical' Foundation of Authority," *Cardozo Law Review*, 11, July/August 1990: 919–1045.

Deutsch, N. "Nahman of Bratslav: The Zaddik as Androgyne," in S. Magid (ed.), *God's Voice from the Void: Old and New Studies in Bratslav Hasidism*, Albany, NY: State University of New York Press, 2001.

Döblin, A. *Kleine Schriften I*, A. W. Riley (ed.), Olten-Freiburg i. Br.: Walter, 1985.

Dohm, C. W. v. *Über die bürgerliche Verbesserung der Juden*, Berlin/Stettin: F. Nicolai, 1781.

Efron, J. M. *Defenders of the Race: Jewish Doctors and Race Science in Fin-de-siècle Europe*, New Haven, NC: Yale University Press, 1994.

Eilberg-Schwartz, H. *God's Phallus and Other Problems for Men and Monotheism*, Boston, MA: Beacon Press, 1994.

Elmer, J. *Reading at the Social Limit: Affect, Mass Culture, and Edgar Allan Poe*, Stanford, CA: Stanford University Press, 1995.

Elon, A. *The Pity of It All: A History of the Jews of Germany, 1743–1933*, New York: Metropolitan/Henry Holt: 2002.

Felski, R. "Those Who Disdain Cultural Studies Don't Know What They're Talking About," *The Chronicle of Higher Education*, July 23, 1999: B7.

Fiedler, L. "Cross the Border – Close the Gap," *Playboy*, December 1969: 151, 230, 252–54, 256–58.

Freedman, Jonathan. "Coming Out of the Jewish Closet with Marcel Proust," *GLQ: A Journal of Lesbian and Gay Studies*, 7, 2001: 521–51.

Friedman, M. S. *Martin Buber's Life and Work: The Early Years, 1878–1923*, New York: Dutton, 1981.

Gann, L. H. and P. Duignan, *The Rulers of German Africa, 1884–1914*, Stanford, CA: Stanford University Press, 1977.

Gay, R. *The Jews in Germany*, New Haven, CT: Yale University Press, 1993.

Gilman, S. L. *Difference and Pathology: Stereotypes of Sexuality, Race, and Madness*, Ithaca, NY: Cornell University Press, 1985.

—— *Jewish Self-Hatred: Anti-Semitism and the Hidden Language of the Jews*, Baltimore, MD: Johns Hopkins University Press, 1986.

—— *Jews in Today's German Culture*, Bloomington, IN: Indiana University Press, 1995.

—— *On Blackness without Blacks: Essays on the Image of the Black in Germany,* Boston, MA: G. K. Hall, 1982

—— and K. Remmler (eds) *Reemerging Jewish Culture in Germany: Life and Literature Since 1989,* New York: New York University Press, 1994.

—— and J. D. Zipes (eds) *Yale Companion to Jewish Writing and Thought in German Culture, 1096–1996,* New Haven, CT: Yale University Press, 1997.

Gilroy, P. *The Black Atlantic: Modernity and Double Consciousness,* London: Verso, 1993.

Gordon, M. M. *Assimilation in American Life: The Role of Race, Religion and National Origins,* New York: Oxford University Press, 1964.

Granach, A. *Da geht ein Mensch. Roman eines Lebens,* Munich: Weismann, 1992.

Grimm, R. and J. Hermand (eds) *Blacks and German Culture: Essays,* Madison, WI: University of Wisconsin Press, 1986.

Gronemann, S. "Erinnerungen," unpublished memoir, Leo Baeck Institute, New York, 1948.

—— "Erinnerungen," unpublished memoirs, Central Zionist Archives, Jerusalem, Record Group A135.

Grözinger, K-E. *Kafka and Kabbalah,* trans. S. H. Ray, New York: Continuum, 1994.

Hall, S. "Introduction," in S. Hall and P. du Gay (eds), *Questions of Cultural Identity,* London: Sage, 1996.

—— "Notes on Deconstructing the Popular," quoted in R. Butsch, *The Making of American Audiences: From Stage to Television, 1750–1990,* New York: Cambridge University Press, 2000, pp. 284–85.

Hansen, M. "Foreword," in O. Negt and A. Kluge (eds), *Public Sphere and Experience: Toward an Analysis of the Bourgeois and Proletarian Public Sphere,* trans. P. Labanyi, J. Daniel, and A. Oksiloff, Minneapolis, MN: University of Minnesota Press, 1993.

—— *Babel and Babylon: Spectatorship in American Silent Film,* Cambridge, MA: Harvard University Press, 1991.

Hartman, G. *The Fateful Question of Culture,* New York: Columbia University Press, 1997.

Hellmann, A. "Stall Levy mit *y*– Lustspiel von Anton Herrnfeld. Herrnfeldtheater im Intimen Theater, Bülowstrasse," *Jüdische Rundschau,* December 23, 1925.

Herzog, T. "Hybrids and *Mischlinge*: Translating Anglo-American Cultural Theory into German," *German Quarterly* 70.1, Winter 1997: 1–17.

Hess, J. M. *Jews, Germans and the Claims of Modernity,* New Haven, CT: Yale University Press, 2002.

Heyse, P. "Einleitung," *Deutscher Novellenschatz,* vol. 1. P. Heyse and H. Kurz (eds), München: Oldenbourg, 1871: 5–22.

Hill, C. *The Soul of Wit: Joke Theory from Grimm to Freud,* Lincoln, NE: University of Nebraska Press, 1993, p. 230.

Hirschfeld, M. "Nachwort," *Girl Years,* pp. 163–66.

Hohendahl, P. U. *Building a National Literature, The Case of Germany 1830–1870,* trans. R. B. Franciscono, Ithaca, NY: Cornell University Press, 1989,

Holub, R. *Reception Theory: A Critical Introduction,* London: Methuen, 1984.

Hull, I. V. *Absolute Destruction: Military Culture and the Practices of War in Imperial Germany,* Ithaca, NY: Cornell University Press, 2005.

Isenschmid, A. "Ein fast neuer Maxim Biller," *Die Zeit*, March 11, 2004. Available from http://www.zeit.de (accessed March 16, 2004).

Jaeger, A. "'Nichts Jüdisches wird uns fremd sein.' Zur Geschichte der Prager *Selbstwehr*, 1907–38," *Aschkenas: Zeitschrift für Geschichte und Kultur der Juden*, vol. 15, no. 1, 2005: 151–207.

Jarausch, K. "Toward a Social History of Experience," *Central European History*, vol. 22, September/December 1989: 427–43.

Jelavich, P. "'Am I Allowed to Amuse Myself Here?' The German Bourgeoisie Confronts Early Film," in S. Marchand and D. Lindenfeld (eds), *Germany at the Fin de Siècle: Culture, Politics, and Ideas*, Baton Rouge, LA: Louisiana University Press, 2004, p. 249.

—— "Berlin Yiddish theater," E-mail (January 30, 2000).

Jofen, J. *The Jewish Mystic in Kafka*, New York: Peter Lang, 1987.

Jungmann, M. *Erinnerungen eines Zionisten*, Jerusalem: Mass, 1959.

—— Papers. Central Zionist Archives, Record Group A/41.

Kadison, L. and J. Buloff (with I. Genn) *On Stage, Off Stage: Memories of a Lifetime in the Yiddish Theatre*, Cambridge, MA: Harvard University Press, 1992.

Kafka, F. *Brief an den Vater*, Frankfurt: Fischer, 1992.

—— *Briefe: 1902–1924*, M. Brod (ed.), Frankfurt a. M.: Fischer, 1975.

—— *Briefe an Felice und andere Korrespondenz aus der Verlobungszeit*, E. Heller and J. Born (eds), Frankfurt a. M.: Fischer, 1976.

—— *Drucke zu Lebzeiten*, H-G. Koch, W. Kittler and G. Neumann (eds) [2 vols, *Kritische Ausgabe*], Frankfurt a. M.: Fischer, 1994b.

—— ["Einleitungsvortrag über Jargon"], *Nachgelassene Schriften und Fragmente I*, M. Pasley (ed.) [2 vols, *Kritische Ausgabe*], Frankfurt a. M.: Fischer, 1993b, pp. 188–93.

—— *Hochzeitungsvorbereitungen auf dem Land und andere Prosa aus dem Nachlaß*, M. Brod (ed.), Frankfurt a. M.: Fischer, 1953.

—— *Nachgelassene Schriften und Fragmente I*, M. Pasley (ed.) [2 vols, *Kritische Ausgabe*], Frankfurt a. M.: Fischer, 1993.

—— *Nachgelassene Schriften und Fragmente II*, J. Schillemeit (ed.) [2 vols, *Kritische Ausgabe*], Frankfurt a. M.: Fischer, 1993a.

—— *Original-Manuskript: Kafka, Franz: Die Verwandlung*, Reihe Oxforder Quarthefte, Basel and Frankfurt a. M.: Stroemfeld, 2003.

—— *Tagebücher, 1910–1923*, M. Brod (ed.), Frankfurt a. M.: Fischer, 1983.

—— *Tagebücher*, H-G. Koch, M. Müller, and M. Pasley (eds) [3 vols, *Kritische Ausgabe*], Frankfurt a. M.: Fischer, 1990.

—— *Zur Frage der Gesetze und andere Schriften aus dem Nachlaß*, H-G. Koch (ed.), Frankfurt a. M.: Fischer, 1994a.

——/M. Brod *Eine Freundschaft. Briefwechsel*, M. Pasley (ed.), 2 vols, Frankfurt a. M.: Fischer, 1989.

Kalmar, I. D. and D. J. Penslar (eds) *Orientalism and the Jews*, Waltham, MA: Brandeis University Press, 2005.

Kämmerling, R. "Biller-Streit: Kunstperson – Was den Fall Maxim Biller so kompliziert macht," *Frankfurter Allgemeine Zeitung*, April 22, 2003. Available from http://www.faz.de (accessed April 26, 2003).

—— [Review of M. Biller's *Esra*], *Frankfurter Allgemeine Zeitung*, March 1, 2003. Available from http://www.faz.de (accessed March 7, 2003).

Kaplan, M. A. (ed.) *Jewish Daily Life in Germany, 1618–1945*, New York: Oxford University Press, 2005.

—— *The Making of the Jewish Middle Classes: Women, Family, and Identity in Imperial Germany*, New York: Oxford University Press, 1991.

Kaufmann, F. M. *Vier Essais über ostjüdische Dichtung und Kultur*, Berlin: Welt-Verlag, 1919.

Kleeblatt, N. (ed.) *Too Jewish? Challenging Traditional Identities*, New Brunswick, NJ: Rutgers University Press, 1996.

Klemperer, V. *Curriculum Vitae: Jugend um 1900*, 2 vols, Berlin: Aufbau, 1989.

Kniesche, T. "Das deutsch-jüdische-amerikanische Dreieck: 'Amerika' als anderer Schauplatz in der zeitgenössischen deutsch-jüdischen Literatur," in J. Vogt and A. Stephan (eds), *Das Amerika der Autoren: Von Kafka bis 09/11*, Munich: Fink, 2006, pp. 337–64.

Kugler, A. [Review of N. O. Body, *Aus eines Mannes Mädchenjahren*], *Die Tageszeitung*, March 8, 1994: 24.

Kun, J. *Audiotopia: Music, Race, and America*, Berkeley, CA: University of California Press, 2005.

Lappin, E. (ed.) *Jewish Voices, German Words*, trans. K. Winston, North Haven, CT: Catbird Press, 1994.

Large, D. C. "'Out with the Ostjuden': The Scheunenviertel Riots in Berlin, November 1923" in W. Bergmann, H. W. Smith, and C. Hoffmann (eds), *Exclusionary Violence: Antisemitic Riots in Modern German History*, Ann Arbor, MI: University of Michigan Press, 2002.

Lessing, T. *Der jüdische Selbsthaß*, Berlin: Matthes und Seitz, 1984.

Levin, T. Y. "Ciphers of Utopia: Critical Theory and the Dialectics of Technological Inscription," unpublished PhD dissertation, Yale University, 1991.

Levine, G. "Yiddish Publishing Activities in Berlin and the Crisis in Eastern European Jewish Culture," *Year Book of the Leo Baeck Institute*, 42, 1997: 85–108.

Levine, L. *Highbrow/Lowbrow: The Emergence of Cultural Hierarchy in America*, Cambridge, MA: Harvard University Press, 1990.

Lowenstein, S. M. *Frankfurt on the Hudson: The German-Jewish Community of Washington Heights, 1933–1983*, Detroit, MI: Wayne State University Press, 1989.

Luz, E. *Parallels Meet: Religion and Nationalism in the Early Zionist Movement (1882–1904)*, Philadelphia, PA: Jewish Publication Society, 1988.

Lyotard, J-F. *Le différend*, Paris: Minuit, 1983.

M.S. [Binjamin Segel], "Ein jüdisches Überbrettl in Galizien," *Ost und West*, December 1902: columns 847–52.

Marx, P. "Im Schatten der Theatergeschichte? Ein Überblick zur Forschung zum jüdischen Theater im deutschsprachigen Raum," *IASL Online. Eine elektronische Zeitschrift für literatur- und kulturwissenschaftliche Rezensionen und Foren*, March 27, 2001. Available from http://www.iasl.uni-muenchen.de (accessed July 15, 2006).

Maurer, T. *Ostjuden in Deutschland 1918–1933*, Hamburg: Hans Christians, 1986,

—— "Partnersuche und Lebensplanung. Heiratsannoncen als Quelle für die Sozial- und Mentalitätsgeschichte der Juden in Deutschland," in P. Freimark, A. Janowski, and I. S. Lorenz (eds), *Juden in Deutschland: Emanzipation, Integration, Verfolgung und Vernichtung: 25 Jahre Institut für die Geschichte der deutschen Juden*, Hamburg: Hans Christians, 1991, pp. 344–74.

Meiring, K. *Die christlich-jüdische Mischehe in Deutschland, 1840–1933*, Hamburg: Dölling & Galitz, 1998.

Meisels, S. "Zur Geschichte des jüdischen Theaters," *Ost und West*, August/September 1908: columns 509–26.

Mendes-Flohr, P. *Divided Passions: Jewish Intellectuals and the Experience of Modernity*, Detroit, MI: Wayne State University Press, 1991.

—— and Reinharz, J. (eds) *The Jew in the Modern World: A Documentary History*, 2nd edn, New York: Oxford University Press, 1995.

Merten, J. [Review of N. O. Body, *Aus eines Mannes Mädchenjahren*], *Berliner Morgenpost*, January 23, 1994.

Miller, T., N. Govil, J. McMurria, and R. Maxwell *Global Hollywood*, London: British Film Institute, 2001.

Modleski, T. *Loving With a Vengeance: Mass-Produced Fantasies for Women*, Hamden, CT: Archon Books, 1982.

Mosse, G. *German Jews* Beyond *Judaism*, Cincinnati, OH: Hebrew Union College Press, 1985.

—— *Nationalism and Sexuality: Middle-Class Morality and Sexual Norms in Modern Europe*, New York: H. Fertig, 1985.

Mosse, W. E. and A. Paucker (eds) *Deutsches Judentum in Krieg und Revolution, 1916–1923*, Tübingen: Mohr, 1971.

Nemitz, K. "Von 'Heißspornen' und Brauseköpfen," in M. Nagel (ed.), *Zwischen Selbstbehauptung und Verfolgung. Deutsch-jüdische Zeitungen von der Aufklärung bis zum Nationalsozialismus*, Hildesheim: Olms, 2002.

Neumann, B. "Der Blick des großen Alexander, die jüdische Assimilation und die 'kosmische Verfügbarkeit des Weibes': Franz Kafkas letzter Roman *Das Schloß* als das Ende einer 'neuen Kabbala'?" *Deutsche Vierteljahrsschrift für Literaturwissenschaft und Geistesgeschichte*, 2005: 307–40.

Niger, S. *Shalom Ash zayn lebn zayne verk: biyografye, opshatsungen, polemik, briv, bibliyografye*, New York: S. Niger bukh-komitet baym Alveltlekhn Yidishn Kultur-kongres, 1960.

Nolden, T. *Junge jüdische Literatur: Konzentrisches Schreiben in der Gegenwart*, Würzburg: Königshausen & Neumann, 1995.

Opet-Fuß, M. "Johann Reuchlin. Roman," *Israelitisches Familienblatt*, installments beginning December 14, 1933.

—— "Judentum und Pazifismus," *Jüdisch-liberale Zeitung*, January 21, 1931: 4.

—— "Jüdischer Sport in der Gegenwart," *Israelitisches Familienblatt*, January 18, 1934, supplement, n.p.

Oring, E. *Jokes and Their Relations*, Lexington, KY: University of Kentucky Press, 1992.

Otte, M. "A World of Their Own? Bourgeois Encounters in Berlin's *Jargon* Theaters, 1890–1920," in S. Marchand and D. Lindenfeld (eds), *Germany at the Fin de Siècle: Culture, Politics, and Ideas*, Baton Rouge, LA: Louisiana State University Press, 2004.

—— "Eine Welt für sich? Bürger im Jargontheater von 1890 bis 1920," in A. Gotzmann, R. Liedtke, and T. van Rahden (eds), *Juden, Bürger, Deutsche: Zur Geschichte von Vielfalt und Differenz, 1800–1933*, Tübingen: Mohr, 2001, pp. 121–46.

Peck, J. M. *Being Jewish in the New Germany*, Rutgers: Rutgers University Press, 2006.

Peterson, B. O. *History, Fiction and Germany: Writing the Nineteenth-Century Nation*, Detroit, MI: Wayne State University Press, 2005.

—— "On the Frankfurt School and German Studies," E-mail (3 April, 1997).

Peukert, D. *The Weimar Republic The Crisis of Classical Modernity*, trans. R. Deveson, New York: Hill and Wang, 1993.

Pinski, D. *Eisik Scheftel. Ein jüdisches Arbeiterdrama in drei Akten*, trans. M. Buber, Berlin: Jüdischer Verlag, 1905.

Politzer, H. *Frank Kafka. Parable and Paradox*, Ithaca, NY: Cornell University Press, 1962.

Presbar, R. "Vorwort" to N. O. Body, *Aus eines Mannes Mädchenjahren*, pp. 2–3.

—— "A Protest against Antisemitism," *The New York Times*, January 16, 1921: 30.

Rabinbach, A. "Between Enlightenment and Apocalypse: Benjamin, Bloch and Modern German Jewish Messianism," *New German Critique*, 1985, no. 34: 78–124.

Radway, J. A. *Reading the Romance: Women, Patriarchy, and Popular Literature*, 2nd edn, Chapel Hill, NC: University of North Carolina Press, 1991.

Reichl, S. and M. Stein (eds) *Cheeky Fictions: Laughter and the Postcolonial*, Amsterdam and New York: Rodopi, 2005.

Reinharz, J. *Chaim Weizmann: The Making of a Zionist Leader*, New York: Oxford University Press, 1985.

Remmler, K. "Encounters Across the Void: Rethinking Approaches to German-Jewish Symbioses," in J. Zipes and L. Morris (eds), *Unlikely History: The Changing Face of the German-Jewish Symbiosis, 1945–2000*, New York: Palgrave, 2002.

—— "Maxim Biller. Das Schreiben als 'Counter-Memory,'" in N. O. Eke and H. Steinecke (eds), *Shoah in der deutschsprachigen Literatur*, Berlin: Erich Schmidt, 2006.

—— and L. Morris (eds) *Contemporary Jewish Writing in Germany: An Anthology*, Lincoln, NE: University of Nebraska Press, 2002.

Riss, H. *Ansätze zu einer Geschichte des jüdischen Theaters in Berlin 1889–1936*, Frankfurt, Berne, New York: Peter Lang, 2000.

Roth, P. *Operation Shylock: A Confession*, New York: Simon & Schuster, 1993.

Rothberg, M. *Traumatic Realism: The Demands of Holocaust Representation*, Minneapolis, MN: University of Minnesota Press, 2000.

Schach, F. "Der deutsch-jüdische Jargon," *Ost und West*, March 1901a: columns 179–90.

—— "Das jüdische Theater, sein Wesen und seine Geschichte," *Ost und West*, May 1901b: columns 351–52, 356, 357–58.

Schäfer, B. and I. Rubin (eds) *Theodor Herzl, Briefe 1903 – Juli 1904*, vol. 7, Frankfurt a. M./Berlin: Propyläen, 1996.

Schmidt, J. "Language, Mythology, and Enlightenment: Historical Notes on Horkheimer and Adorno's *Dialectic of Enlightenment*," *Social Research*, 65, Winter 1998: 807–38.

Schneider, W. [Review of M. Biller, *Bernsteintage*], *Neue Zürcher Zeitung*, April 13, 2004. Available from http://www.lexis-nexis.com (accessed February 25, 2007).

Scholem, G. "Against the Myth of the German-Jewish Dialogue," in W. J. Dannhauser (ed.), *On Jews and Judaism in Crisis*, New York: Schocken, 1976.

—— *Mi-berlin li-yerushalayim* [From Berlin to Jerusalem], expanded Hebrew edn, Tel Aviv: Am Oved, 1982.

—— "–Und alles ist Kabbala": Gershom Scholem im Gespräch mit Jörg Drews, Munich: dtv, 1980.

—— Walter Benjamin: The Story of a Friendship, trans. H. Zohn, Philadelphia, PA: Jewish Publication Society, 1981,

Seyhan, A. "Lost in Translation: Re-Membering the Mother Tongue in Emine Sevgi Özdamar's Das Leben ist eine Karawanserei," German Quarterly, 69, 1996: 414–26.

Simon, H. "Wer war N. O. Body?" in H. Simon (ed.), Aus eines Mannes Mädchenjahren, Berlin: Edition Hentrich, 1993, pp. 167–246.

Sinakowski, A. Das Verhör, Berlin: BasisDruck, 1991.

Smith, W. D. The German Colonial Empire, Chapel Hill, NC: University of North Carolina Press, 1978.

—— The Ideological Origins of Nazi Imperialism, New York: Oxford University Press, 1986.

Sorkin, D. "Emancipation and Assimilation – Two Concepts and Their Application to German-Jewish History", in Year Book of the Leo Baeck Institute 35, 1990: 27–33.

Sprengel, P. Populäres jüdisches Theater in Berlin von 1877 bis 1933, Berlin: Haude & Spener, 1997.

—— Scheunenviertel-Theater: Jüdische Schauspieltruppen und jiddische Dramatik in Berlin (1900–1918), Berlin: Fannei und Walz, 1995.

Stach, R. Kafka. Die Jahre der Entscheidungen, Frankfurt a. M.: Fischer, 2002.

—— Kafka: The Decisive Years, trans. S. Frisch, New York: Harcourt, 2005.

Steinecke, H. "'Deutsch-jüdische' Literatur heute. Die Generation nach der Shoah. Zur Einführung," in S. L. Gilman and H. Steinecke (eds), Deutsch-jüdische Literatur der neunziger Jahre, Berlin: Erich Schmidt Verlag, 2002.

Steinlauf, M. C. "Fear of Purim: Y. L. Peretz and the Canonization of Yiddish Theater," Jewish Social Studies, new series, 1, Spring 1995: 44–65.

Stern, F. "The Integration of the Jews in Nineteenth-Century Germany," Year Book of the Leo Baeck Institute, 20, 1975: 79–83.

Strassfeld, M. Jewish Holidays. A Guide and Commentary, New York: Harper and Row, 1985.

Strauss, W. A. On the Threshold of a New Kabbalah: Kafka's Later Tales, New York: Peter Lang, 1988.

—— "Trying to Mend the Broken Vessels," in A. Udoff (ed.), Kafka's Contextuality, Staten Island, NY: Gordian Press, and Baltimore, MD: Baltimore Hebrew College, 1986.

Tiefenbrun, R. Moment of Torment: An Interpretation of Franz Kafka's Short Stories, Carbondale, IL: Southern Illinois University Press, 1973.

Uricchio, W. and R. Pearson Reframing Culture: The Case of the Vitagraph Quality Films, Princeton, NJ: Princeton University Press, 1992.

"Urteile der Presse über die Jüdischen Volksliederabende," Ost und West, December 1912: columns 1169–90 and 1197–1120.

van Rahden, T. Juden und andere Breslauer. Die Beziehungen zwischen Juden, Protestanten und Katholiken in einer deutschen Großstadt von 1860 bis 1925, Göttingen: Vandenhoeck und Ruprecht, 2000.

Vida, S. [Review of N. O. Body, Aus eines Mannes Mädchenjahren], DeutschlandRadio, 28 March, 1994, 4:10 p.m. to 4.30 p.m.

Wagenbach, K. Franz Kafka in Selbstzeugnissen und Bilddokumenten, Reinbek: Rowohlt, 1964.

Walter, D. *Antisemitische Kriminalität und Gewalt: Judenfeindschaft in der Weimarer Republik*, Bonn: Dietz, 1999.

Wertheimer, J. "The German-Jewish Experience: Toward a Useable Past," *American Jewish Archives*, 40, November 1988: 417–23.

—— *Unwelcome Strangers: East European Jews in Imperial Germany*, New York: Oxford University Press, 1987.

West, J. L., III *American Authors and the Literary Marketplace since 1900*, Philadelphia, PA: University of Pennsylvania Press, 1988.

White, H. *Metahistory: The Historical Imagination in Nineteenth Century Europe*, Baltimore, MD: Johns Hopkins University Press, 1973.

Whitfield, S. *In Search of American Jewish Culture*, Hanover, NH: University Press of New England, 1999.

Winz, L. Papers, Central Zionist Archives, Jerusalem, Record group A136.

Wisse, R. R. *The Schlemiel as Modern Hero*, Chicago, IL: University of Chicago Press, 1971.

Wolfson, E. *Circle in the Square: Studies in the Use of Gender in Kabbalistic Symbolism*, Albany, NY: State University of New York Press, 1995.

Wolzogen, E. von. "Das jüdische Theater in Amerika," *Selbstwehr* (Prag), 5, October 27, 1911: n.p.

Zipes, J. D. (ed.) *The Operated Jew: Two Tales of Anti-Semitism*, New York: Routledge, 1991.

Zischler, H. *Kafka geht ins Kino*, Hamburg: Rowohlt, 1996.

INDEX

actors, 16, 21–22, 78, 92
Adler, J. 19
Adorno, T. W. 5–6, 73, 75, 87–89
Africans 28, 36–37; *see also* Blacks
Ahad Ha'am 7, 30
Aleichem, Sholem 15
Ansky, S. 18, 20, 24, 25, 93
anti-defamation 67, 68; *see also*
  Centralverein
antisemitism 12, 17, 31, 62, 64–65,
  69, 82
Arendt, H. 31, 36, 94
Armenian genocide 79
asceticism 50–51, 56, 58
Asch, S. 15, 20, 21, 22, 23, 93
assimilation 2, 7, 11, 13, 31, 33, 61–63,
  75, 89, 100; *see also* self-hatred
audience *see* marketing and audience

Baer, K. M. 8, 40–45
Bauer, F. 8, 25–26, 51, 56, 94
Barbin, H. 41–42, 47–48, 96
Berlin 1, 12–13, 17, 26, 64, 70–71, 94;
  see also Scheunenviertel *and* theater
Bhabha, H. 8, 40, 96
Biale, D. 31, 49, 94
Bildung 5, 88; *see also* Enlightenment
Biller, Maxim 77–78, 100–102;
  "Finkelstein's Fingers" 76–82; *Esra*
  75, 76, 79, 84, 85
Birmingham School 2, 6, 48, 89; *see
  also* cultural studies
Blacks 6, 27, 34–37, 77; *see also*
  Africans

Boyarin, D. 31, 32, 56, 99
Brod, M. 49, 50, 86
Buber, Martin 9, 11, 14, 24–25, 49, 59,
  93, 97, 100
Butler, J. 4, 30, 48, 77–78, 86–89, 103

Centralverein deutscher Staatsbürger
  jüdischen Glaubens 62, 68–69
circumcision 58
class 6, 7, 18–20, 41, 45, 62, 63, 72, 96;
  see also middle classes
colonialism 8, 28–29, 35, 41, 95
comedy 16–20, 30, 46, 49; *see also*
  humor
cultural studies 2, 4, 6–7, 10, 48, 90
Cultural Zionism 8, 28, 31, 40, 94

Day of Atonement *see* Yom Kippur
Democratic Faction 31
dissimilation 50
dialect 14, 17, 21, 41, 91
Dybbuk 18, 23–25, 93; *see also*
  Ansky, S.

East European Jewish, 7, 14, 24, 36, 40,
  76
East European Jews *see* Eastern Jews
Eastern Jew 11–14, 18, 22–26, 35–36,
  62, 69, 75, 89
Eilberg-Schwartz, H. 51, 52, 57, 58
Enlightenment 3, 5, 13, 28, 32, 68, 89
eroticism 46, 52, 98; *see also*
  homosexuality
essentialism 3–4, 42, 45, 78, 84, 97

ethnicity 1–3, 79, 81
ethnocentrism 32
film 1,6, 18, 91
Foucault, M. 4, 41, 46–47, 87
Frankfurt School *see* Adorno, T. W.
Freud, Sigmund and Freudianism 41,
    43, 47, 49, 51, 57–58; psychoanalysis
    49, 57, 97

Die Gartenlaube 44, 62
gender 31, 42, 49–51, 57, 59, 76, 79–81;
    anti-feminism 73, 84
German Jews 1–3, 10–13, 23, 41, 62;
    see also Yekkes
God 49–54
Goldfaden, A. 15, 18, 21, 25, 91
Gordin, J. 21, 22, 92
Granach, A. 22, 26, 92, 94
Gronemann, S. 24, 33, 93, 95
Grözinger, K-E. 49, 58

Habima 24
Hall, S. 2, 4, 75, 88
Hansen, M. 6
Hasidism 9, 11, 25, 49, 54–55, 59
Hebrew 14, 24
hegemony 2, 7, 85
Heine, H. 31, 86
Herero 36
hermaphroditism 41–46, 48
Herrnfeld theater 16–21, 91–92
Herzl, T. 8, 27, 31–34
Hirschfeld, M. 41, 43, 46, 97
Holiness Code (Leviticus) 50, 54
Holocaust 1, 11, 12, 69, 75, 78, 84–85
homoeroticism *see* homosexuality
homosexuality 41, 49, 51, 56–57
Horkheimer, M. 5–6, 75, 88
humor 7–8, 15, 33, 37, 43, 78, 96; *see
    also* comedy

identity 2–5, 41, 79, 84, 87;
    identification 3, 7, 41, 76, 81, 83
immigrants and immigration 12, 17–19,
    22, 27
intellectuals 1, 6, 13, 87
intermarriage *see* marriage
intertextuality 9, 41, 78
irony and self-irony 8, 16, 18, 27, 41,
    78–81
Israelitisches Familienblatt 9, 14, 34, 43,
    62–65, 69–70, 74, 75

Jettchen Gebert 71, 74
Jewish nationalism 13, 28–29; *see also*
    Zionism
Jewish Studies 3, 87
Judaism *see* religion, Jewish
Jungmann, M. 33–34, 36, 95

Kabbalah 49, 58, 97, 98
Kafka, F. 1, 2, 7, 9, 11, 16, 18–21, 23,
    25–26, 65, 85, 97, 101; and Judaism
    49–59, *The Castle* 59; "The
    Judgment" 51–56, 59, 99; "The
    Metamorphosis" 51, 56, 97; "In the
    Penal Colony" 56; *The Trial* 55–56,
    97
kitsch versus art 5, 17–20, 46, 62, 75,
    85, 91; *shund* 5, 19–20
klezmer 23, 27

Langer, Jiří 9, 49, 58
Liberal Judaism 17, 23, 68, 72; *see also*
    Reform Judaism
Lilien, E. M. 14, 25, 37
London 19, 94
Löwy, J. 8–9, 21, 25–26, 49
Lyotard, J. F. 1

magazines 25–26, 34, 57, 72; *see also
    Die Gartenlaube* and *Israelitisches
    Familienblatt* and *Ost und West*
male readers 35, 65, 74
Mann, Thomas 11, 72
marketing and audiences 12–13, 18–19,
    24–26, 33, 37–39, 41–42, 44–45, 71
marriage 49–51, 66–69, 72
masculinity 36, 39, 43, 49–51, 55
masochism 47, 97
mass culture 5, 43, 74–76, 78, 87; *see
    also* popular culture
mass media 2, 5
Mendele (Moykher-Sforim) 16, 23
middle classes 12, 18, 39, 63–64, 90
middlebrow 2, 24, 75, 87
migration *see* immigrants and
    immigration
minority groups 3, 6, 7, 20, 39
Mizrachi Zionism 28–31, 34–35; *see
    also* Zionism
modernism 1, 6, 18
Moses 50–51, 56, 98, 99
Mosse, G. 87, 90, 92, 97, 101
music 18, 23–25, 33

mysticism, Jewish 20, 49, 51, 58; *see also* Kabbalah

Nachman, Reb (of Bratslav) 59–60, 98
nationalism 2, 26, 28–31, 63, 69; *see also* Jewish nationalism
New York City 16, 19, 79, 91
Noah 49, 53, 98
Nordau, M. 15

Opet-Fuß, M. 63–66, 67; "Versöhnung" 64–69
Ost und West 12–15, 22–26
Ostjuden see Eastern Jews

Panizza, O. 39, 42
Pappenheim, Bertha 41, 75, 99
Peretz, I. L. 14–15, 23, 59
performance 3, 4, 5, 9, 16–20, 26, 28–29, 35, 41, 46, 94; performativity, 9, 31, 77–80, 82, 84
Pinski, D. 15, 23
popular culture 2, 5–7, 10, 20, 76
postcolonialism 4, 8, 28–29, 36, 39
postmodernism 47, 78, 84, 87, 88
Prague 1, 2, 19–20, 26, 76, 100
prostitution 20–21, 41, 63, 74

Rabbinic Judaism 5, 15, 31, 51–54, 68
Rabinbach, A. 87
Radnóti, Miklos 80, 81
Rathenau, Walther 64–66, 69
Realism 15, 71, 76, 83
reception 7, 12–13, 26, 41, 76, 89, 102
Reform Judaism 35; *see also* Liberal Judaism
Reinhardt, Max 21–22, 92
religion, Jewish 2–3, 32, 39, 59, 69, 97; *see also* God
Renaissance, Jewish 14, 34
respectability 18, 22, 35, 45
rhetoricity 6, 9, 11, 41, 69
Roth, Philip 78
Russia 19, 35, 54–55, 90

Salomonski, M. 63, 64, 72; "Die geborene Tugendreich" 71–75
satire 16, 31–36, 75

Schach, F. 14–17, 22, 89
Scheunenviertel 8, 18, 21–22, 26, 70–74, 93; *see also* Berlin
schlemiel 30–31, 94
Scholem, Gershom 1, 7, 20, 49, 89, 97
Schreber, Daniel Paul 57, 58
self-hatred 2, 9, 12, 41–42, 48, 97
shund *see* kitsch
Simplicissimus 33, 39
stereotyping 11, 13, 15–16, 19–20, 28, 35–37, 78, 81, 100
symbiosis 1, 11, 75–76, 85

Talmud *see* Rabbinic Judaism
theater, Yiddish 12–13, 33, 49, 92, 94; Berlin Yiddish theater 15–27; *see also* Habima *and* Herrnfeld theater *and* varieté
theory 3–4, 10, 76
translation (from Yiddish) 14–15, 21, 23–25, 92
Trivialliteratur see kitsch

Uganda controversy 27, 31, 34–35
United States 1, 16, 18–19, 33, 80

varieté theater 13, 18, 19, 23
Vienna 19, 91
violence 31, 36, 70–71, 74

Western Jewish 11–13, 85, 88; *see also* Eastern Jews
Williams, R. 2, 6
Winz, Leo 14, 20–25, 33, 34
Wolfson, E. 50
women 6, 41, 46, 52, 53, 55–56, 66–68, 74
working-class *see* class

yekke (or *Yekke*) 7–8, 16, 37–38
Yiddish language 13, 14, 16, 23
Yiddish theater *see* theater
Yom Kippur 55, 56, 59, 66, 72

Zionism 15, 17, 31–35, 36–39, 50, 69; *see also* Cultural Zionism *and* Mizrachi Zionism